Teacher Education Online

Teacher Education Online

A Practical Guide for Instruction

**Kathleen A. Boothe and
Marla J. Lohmann**

BLOOMSBURY ACADEMIC
NEW YORK • LONDON • OXFORD • NEW DELHI • SYDNEY

BLOOMSBURY ACADEMIC

Bloomsbury Publishing Inc, 1359 Broadway, New York, NY 10018, USA
Bloomsbury Publishing Plc, 50 Bedford Square, London, WC1B 3DP, UK
Bloomsbury Publishing Ireland, 29 Earlsfort Terrace, Dublin 2, D02 AY28, Ireland

BLOOMSBURY, BLOOMSBURY ACADEMIC and the Diana logo are
trademarks of Bloomsbury Publishing Plc

First published in the United States of America 2025

Copyright © Kathleen A. Boothe, Marla J. Lohmann, 2025

For legal purposes the Acknowledgments on pp. ix–x constitute an
extension of this copyright page.

Cover design by Dustin Watson
Cover image © istock/Kateryna Onyshchuk

All rights reserved. No part of this publication may be: i) reproduced or transmitted in
any form, electronic or mechanical, including photocopying, recording or by means of
any information storage or retrieval system without prior permission in writing from the
publishers; or ii) used or reproduced in any way for the training, development or operation
of artificial intelligence (AI) technologies, including generative AI technologies. The rights
holders expressly reserve this publication from the text and data mining exception as per
Article 4(3) of the Digital Single Market Directive (EU) 2019/790.

Bloomsbury Publishing Inc does not have any control over, or responsibility for, any
third-party websites referred to or in this book. All internet addresses given in this
book were correct at the time of going to press. The author and publisher regret
any inconvenience caused if addresses have changed or sites have ceased
to exist, but can accept no responsibility for any such changes.

Library of Congress Cataloging-in-Publication Data is available

ISBN: HB: 978-1-5381-9452-2
PB: 978-1-5381-9453-9
ePub: 978-1-5381-9454-6
ePDF: 979-8-7651-5506-6

Typeset by Integra Software Services Pvt. Ltd.

For product safety related questions contact productsafety@bloomsbury.com.

To find out more about our authors and books visit www.bloomsbury.com
and sign up for our newsletters.

Kathy and Marla would like to dedicate this book to all of the teacher educators out there who are doing their best every day to support current and future PK–12 teachers. We hope this book supports you in your online instructional journey.

Contents

Acknowledgments ix

Introduction 1

1 Engaging Learners in Teacher Education Coursework 11
2 Building Online Learning Communities 35
3 Asynchronous Discussion Boards That Enhance Student Learning 57
4 Implementing Remote Observations of Field Experiences into Online Programming 85
5 Authentic Assessment as an Instructional Practice 107
6 Assessing Student Learning 131
7 The Reflective Practitioner 147
8 Creating a Work-Life Balance When You Are Always Connected 167

Conclusion 185

Appendix A: "We Do" Responses from Kathy and Marla 187
Appendix B: "You Do" Examples 196
Appendix C: ADA Compliance 201
Appendix D: Universal Design for Learning 204
Appendix E: Trauma-Informed Instruction in Higher Education 207

Appendix F: Artificial Intelligence in the Online Classroom 210
Appendix G: Our Favorite Things 216
Appendix H: Additional Resources We Recommend 218
Index 221
About the Authors 223

Acknowledgments

What a fun time we had writing this book. It was definitely a project that has been a dream of ours for years—we started talking about this book during the COVID-19 shutdowns, when we were frequently being asked by colleagues for advice on online instruction. At that time, we did not yet feel like we had enough knowledge to share with others to write an entire book—we felt confident in writing lots of articles and book chapters about online teaching but were not yet ready for a book! As we wrote this book, we were reminded that we are in no way perfect in the world of online teaching but that we do have a lot of good instructional practices in our courses and a significant amount of experience with virtual instruction. Throughout the book-writing journey, we learned even more about each other and discovered that Kathy works much better under pressure, while Marla would be much less stressed if she had started her writing journey early and had more time to think about what to say!

We want to take the next few moments to acknowledge those professional colleagues who have encouraged us, given us ideas, and shared their experiences—whether they know it or not! Specifically, some of our most important (and favorite) colleagues—Dr. Frank Dykes, Jayanna Greenwood, Kathy Johnson, Dr. Adam Moore, Dr. Ruby Owiny, Dr. Kate Shannon, Dr. Christala Smith, Dr. Matthew Taylor, and Dr. Jennifer Walker. Many of the activities and other items that we mention throughout the book, tweaked to work for us and our classes, have come from those named above. In addition, these people motivate us and inspire us to be better teacher educators every day—when you surround yourself with amazing colleagues, you constantly strive to improve!

We also want to thank our students, because without them we would not have jobs! But seriously, we would definitely not be the teachers we are today without their feedback! Sometimes their feedback hurts to hear (and we have certainly been known to cry a few times over student feedback), but it has also helped us to grow as teacher educators. So, current and former students, if you happen to be reading this book (and unless you now teach at a university, we doubt you are), thank you for sharing your thoughts with us.

And last (but not least), we want to give professional thanks to Dr. Lyndal Bullock, or Dr. B as we call him. He was our advisor in our PhD program, and we have him to thank for our current careers. We are the professional teacher educators we are today thanks to his guidance, instruction, and feedback. Thank you, Dr. B!

Kathy would also like to give a shout-out to her husband, Clark, who put up with her mood swings (aka grumpiness) and never-ending late-night and weekend book writing. He provided support and encouragement whenever she needed it, and she cannot imagine her life without his support! Kathy also wants to thank Marla for working with her on our first book project together. We have written many articles and presented together at many conferences, but this was a new learning experience, and Kathy is so glad to have been able to work with her on this project!

Marla would like to thank her family for their never-ending support of her career and her desire to support teachers and schools. Mark, Abigail, Charlotte, Esther, and Abraham—you all are amazing, and I am completely and absolutely blessed that you are my family! Thank you, thank you, thank you! And, great news—the book is written now, which means a "book birthday party" is coming soon! I can't wait to celebrate the launch of this book with cupcakes and sparkling juice! Marla also wants to thank Kathy for putting up with her Type A tendencies—I am glad we wrote this together!

Finally, thank you to everyone who purchased this book and is taking the time to read our work. We know you could have chosen any number of online teaching books. We appreciate that you have chosen this one to read, and we hope that you are able to take some new strategies and ideas from this book.

—Kathy and Marla

Introduction

We have both taught online for almost a decade. At first, we were both hesitant to teach in the virtual classroom and believed that online learning is not effective. Over time, our views have changed and we have come to love being fully online teacher educators, and we believe that well-designed online courses are ideal learning environments for many students. Writing this book has been one of our goals for several years. During COVID, many of our colleagues got their first experiences with teaching online, and some of them came to us for advice on how to support students in the virtual classroom. In this book, we share the advice we have given friends over the years—we hope it helps each of you just as it has helped them.

Author Positionality

Before we dig into the "meat" of this book and share our online teaching advice, we would like to share our stories. The academics in us know that researcher positionality matters in understanding the context of what is being presented. So we want to share our author positionality with you. We both began our online teaching journey at about the same time. In those first few years, we talked almost daily to share stories and experiences, as well as to help one another navigate the realities of online teaching. Despite the fact that our online teaching journeys began at about the same time, our stories are different.

We all know students, or maybe we were even one of those students, who do just enough to get by and pass the course. They wait until the very last minute and do the bare minimum. Kathy admits she was that student once upon a time in her educational career. When she began teaching online, she vowed that she did not want her students to be *that* student. She wanted her students to enjoy coming to class. She wanted to take them out of their comfort zone and have them try new and engaging tools, etc. She wanted them to feel like they were not alone, that they were part of a team. After eight years of teaching fully online, she believes she is finally getting there! She is by no means an expert, but she tries her best to accomplish those tasks in her teaching. For the most part, many of her students do seem engaged and have been appreciative of the authentic assessments incorporated into her courses.

During her doctoral studies, Marla's husband got a job offer that moved her family overseas for two years. Luckily, Marla was ready to do her dissertation at the time, and her advisor agreed to a remote research project (which was not common in 2012)! She proposed her research project two days before getting on a plane to move, conducted an online survey for her dissertation study, and defended her dissertation via Skype. That early experience with online learning prepared Marla for later taking a full-time remote professor position after her return to living in the United States. When Marla first began that position, she had four children under the age of eight and was looking for a professional opportunity that would allow her the flexibility to work from home with children at home. At the time, she intended to work remotely for a few years and then find a more traditional academic position once all of her children entered school. Now, nine years later, she cannot imagine not teaching online. Throughout this book, you will find that Marla frequently talks about her work-life balance as she does her best to meet the needs of her family, her students, and her university.

Our Beliefs About Teaching and Learning

At this time, we also want to share with you our personal and professional beliefs about teaching and learning. We know that our beliefs impact how we approach our classroom instruction and how we approached the writing of this book. With that in mind, we believe it is only fair to share those beliefs with you so that you know where we were coming from when writing this book. Simply put, we believe the following:

- All people have the ability to learn.
- Online learning is an effective method of instruction.
- Some students need additional learning supports in order to be successful.

- Learning styles are a myth, but learning preferences are real.
- A universally designed classroom is inherently designed to meet a variety of learning needs and preferences.
- Good teachers use evidence-based instructional practices.
- Teachers must be lifelong learners who are willing to challenge their own beliefs and continue growing in their personal and professional knowledge and skills.
- Teacher educators need to use both direct and explicit instruction, while also facilitating student learning.
- Both teachers and students must be actively engaged in the course in order for true learning to occur.
- As teacher educators, we are both teaching content and modeling good instructional practices in our courses. Our students learn the material we teach, but they also learn how to teach by observing us. With this in mind, we must use high-quality instructional practices.
- Teachers are responsible for creating a learning environment that ensures all learners have access to what they need to learn. Learners are responsible for utilizing what is provided by the teacher and learning the content.
- Teaching is the best job in the world!!!!!

Preview of the Book

As teachers, we know that it is important to give students a preview of what they are going to learn. In the following paragraphs, we offer a brief glimpse into each of the chapters. As you read through the book, know that we do realize that some of the activities are not suited for all students. It is important that you refer to individual student accommodations and modify activities as needed for those who struggle with issues that may keep them from successfully completing some of your activities. More on ADA (Americans with Disabilities Act) compliance and meeting the needs of students with disabilities, including those who are neurodiverse, can be found in Appendices C and D.

Each of the book chapters is designed to be a stand-alone reading. While we highly recommend reading the entire book (we worked very hard writing it and sincerely hope people read it!), you don't necessarily need to read each chapter in order. Select the chapter that most intrigues you or meets your most immediate need to read first and then go back and read the other chapters.

Each of the chapters is set up similarly. The chapter opens with three myths about the topic to be discussed, followed by an explanation of why those concepts are myths. Next, we move to the "I Do" section of the chapter, where we offer suggested strategies and tools that are backed by research and that we personally find to support our own online teaching. In this section, we share our own stories and personal experiences. The third section of each chapter is the "We Do" section in which we offer a vignette and discussion questions for you to consider. If you are working through this book in a book study with colleagues, we highly recommend completing the "We Do" section together. To support your learning in this section, we have included Appendix A at the end of the book. In this appendix, we offer our own answers to some of the questions posed in the "We Do" section of each chapter. We suggest that you first consider the question being posed, create your own response to the question, and then look at our response to compare with yours. Finally, every chapter closes with a "You Do" section in which you are asked to apply the concepts presented in the chapter to your own teaching. At the end of the book, we offer eight appendices to share additional information. Each of the appendices is described in the Conclusion section of the book, and you can find them listed in the Table of Contents.

In addition, we want to take this opportunity to mention that this book is in no way a comprehensive guide to online teacher preparation. There is so much to know beyond the scope of this book. As we wrote this manuscript, we had to make a lot of hard decisions and select the information that we believe new (or fairly new) online teacher educators should know.

We also want to caution you about getting overwhelmed as you read. We present a lot of ideas in this book, but we would never expect an instructor to begin implementing all of them at once. Start small! Choose one idea, implement it, perfect it, and then add another idea.

Explanation of Terms

At this time, we want to share a brief explanation of how we use a few terms in this book to ensure that we are all on the same page as you read. We use the terms "online," "remote," and "virtual" interchangeably to indicate online coursework and teaching online. We acknowledge that you may be teaching online courses from your on-campus office and don't necessarily feel "remote," but you are remotely located from your students. We have elected to use the word "students" to talk about the pre-service and in-service teachers who take courses in teacher education programs. We have done this because, as teacher educators, they are our students. We apologize in advance if this causes any confusion when you think about teacher education students versus the PK–12 students they teach. "College," "university," and "institute of higher education" are used throughout the text to refer to any teaching that occurs outside of PK–12—this book is appropriate for you whether you are at a two-year college, a four-year university, or other postsecondary institution.

As we were writing this book, we had many discussions over the words "authentic assessment" and "assessment." We each had differing definitions for what we believe assessments are, but we talked through it and we wanted to make sure you all know that when we say "assessment" or "authentic assessment," we are speaking of any formative or summative assessment. This can include weekly assignments, discussions, and final projects.

The term "instruction" is a word that you may or may not see in the Table of Contents or throughout the book. However, please know that the areas of online teaching we cover are different types of instruction, so our hope is that you will read through this book and assume the entire book is on good instruction in the online classroom.

Artificial Intelligence (AI)

As we write this book in 2024, artificial intelligence (AI) is a hot topic of discussion, and many people believe it will change how we teach and learn in the online classroom. While we do believe there are significant considerations related to AI, especially for technology-based learning like online coursework, we do not think it changes the basic principles of good instruction. And we believe it is still too early to truly know the impact of AI on learning—we see both its promise and the potential problems surrounding its use. In Appendix F, we share additional thoughts and considerations related to AI for online teacher preparation.

Universal Design for Learning

As we noted above in our list of teaching and learning beliefs, we believe that the most effective classrooms, for students from preschool through graduate school, are designed using the Universal Design for Learning (UDL) framework. UDL is an educational approach based on decades of research on learning and brain functioning. Teachers who design and implement instruction within the UDL framework offer multiple means of engagement, multiple means of representation, and multiple means of action and expression. As you read this book, you will notice that we mention UDL in a variety of chapters, and our approach to online teaching is aimed at meeting these three UDL principles. To learn more about UDL and see our list of recommended resources on the topic, please see Appendix D.

Regular and Substantive Feedback

There are two schools of thought on instruction in distance learning. While the idea that an online course is synchronous or asynchronous is important, we also notice that within these two realms there are two more ideas concerning distance learning. One idea is that online programs should be self-paced and include self-instruction, as in correspondence courses. The other idea is that students should be engaged with their learning and that instructors are an integral part of the online environment. The idea of regular and substantive interactions (RSIs) applies to those institutes of higher education that receive Title IV funds, with the understanding that they should be providing an online learning environment in which students are actively engaged in their coursework. According to the Office of Postsecondary Education, Department of Education (2021), as it relates to distance education,

> *For purposes of this definition, substantive interaction is engaging students in teaching, learning, and assessment, consistent with the content under discussion, and also includes at least two of the following—(i) Providing direct instruction; (ii) Assessing or providing feedback on a student's coursework; (iii) Providing information or responding to questions about the content of a course or competency; (iv) Facilitating a group discussion regarding the content of a course or competency; or (v) Other instructional activities approved by the institution's or program's accrediting agency.*

> *(5) An institution ensures regular interaction between a student and an instructor or instructors by, prior to the student's completion of a course or competency—(i) Providing the opportunity for substantive interactions with the student on a predictable and scheduled basis commensurate with the length of time and the amount of content in the course or competency; and (ii) Monitoring the student's academic engagement and success and ensuring that an instructor is responsible for promptly and proactively engaging in substantive interaction with the student when needed on the basis of such monitoring, or upon request by the student.*

What this says to us is that you should be engaging with your students throughout the course by providing scheduled and meaningful feedback and interaction with the students in your online courses. While RSI is not within the main scope of this book, many of the ideas we discuss, along with using the UDL framework, can assist online instructors in meeting many of the requirements of RSI.

Chapter Overviews

Chapter 1 will introduce you to online teaching and what we feel is the most important aspect of getting started—engaging your learners. Online teaching is not just about supplying content in the learning management system (LMS) and being an active participant in your students' learning. With online teaching, there is much more that has to be done behind the scenes and before classes begin. Yes, we know that you have to prepare for your classes when you teach face-to-face, but incorporating engaging practices for online teaching needs to be thoughtfully planned. This chapter will discuss some of the key ways we strive to engage our students at the beginning and throughout the course.

Once you have worked on gaining engaged learners, Chapter 2 will look at ways to build community in the online class. We all know that teaching online can seem lonely, but the same applies to our students. It is important that, as instructors, we purposefully plan ways to build community in our online courses. As with Chapter 1, many of the suggestions we provide in Chapter 2 are things that need to be set up before the course begins and then followed up through the remainder of the class.

We next move on to creating instructional activities in the classroom. Chapter 3 discusses several aspects of asynchronous discussion boards. We have given presentations and written several articles and book chapters on asynchronous discussions, so we knew this had to be a part of our book. In this chapter we will take a look at specific components of setting up the posts as well as ways to change up your discussion prompts. This is the longest chapter in the book, but it is what we work hard on in our own classes, which means we have a lot to share!

As you probably already figured out, this book is about teaching online in teacher education programs, which means that many of you reading this book may be teaching pre-service teachers. This means there is most likely an expectation for students to be in schools observing teachers, volunteering, or even student teaching. With this in mind, we have added Chapter 4 to discuss three key pieces of implementing remote observations in your online program or courses.

Chapters 5 and 6 focus on assessments. Chapter 5 provides you with information on creating authentic assessments as an instructional practice. We focus on three authentic assessments in particular, but you will also find several examples of other types of authentic assessments we use in our classrooms in this chapter, as well as throughout the book. Chapter 6 will then provide the reader with specific ways to effectively assess your learners, including rubrics and specific feedback.

At this point in the book, we have covered information on getting ready for teaching online, building community, and instructional activities that can be incorporated in your courses. The final chapters are all about us, the instructors. Chapter 7 will focus on your being a reflective practitioner and on ways that you can reflect on your teaching and use the information effectively to make changes to your courses. Chapter 8 focuses on creating a work-life balance. While we are definitely no experts in this area, we do strive to create this balance and will offer ways we have managed to do this as well as ideas we have heard from colleagues who do this exceptionally well!

Thank You!

Thank you for taking the time to read this book. We hope that it supports you in your online teaching and that you come to enjoy being a virtual teacher educator just as much as we love it! As you go through the book, we urge you to share your learning and your own online teaching experiences with us. We both use Twitter/X for professional purposes. You can find Kathy at @kah1978 and Marla at @MarlaLohmann. Please use the hashtag #OnlineTeacherPrep and tag both of us in your post.

Reference

Office of Postsecondary Education, Department of Education. (2021). *34CFR600.2 (2021)*. https://www.ecfr.gov/current/title-34/subtitle-B/chapter-VI/part-600/subpart-A/section-600.2

1 Engaging Learners in Teacher Education Coursework

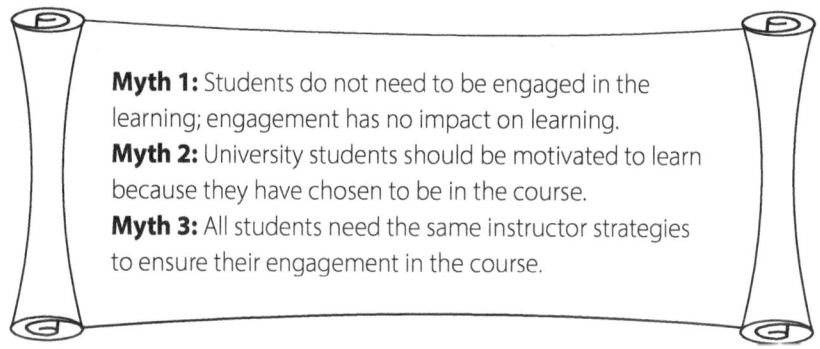

Myth 1: Students do not need to be engaged in the learning; engagement has no impact on learning.
Myth 2: University students should be motivated to learn because they have chosen to be in the course.
Myth 3: All students need the same instructor strategies to ensure their engagement in the course.

Debunking the Myths

As teacher educators with a decade each of online teaching experience, we have a lot of knowledge, and even more opinions, about best practices in virtual teaching. One of the things we have learned over the years is that student engagement is nonnegotiable when teaching online. While engaging learners is vital for face-to-face courses, in our experience it is even more critical in the online classroom where students can easily disconnect from instruction and learning. The reality is that over half of all college students find traditional learning strategies and classroom instruction to be boring and unengaging (Mann & Robinson, 2009)—whether we know it or not, there are students in our courses who are not fully engaged in the learning. While we find our subject area to be incredibly engaging and exciting (if we did not love it, we would not be professors), our students do not always agree. And even if they love the content, they may not be fully engaged due to competing demands on their time or for other reasons.

The term "student engagement" is not well defined in the literature, with various researchers defining it slightly differently (Oele et al., 2017). For our purposes in this chapter, we define it as "student motivation that leads to active student participation in their own learning, including in classwide and individual activities." Simply attending class or completing coursework does not necessarily equate to engagement. Neither does interest in the learning topic when it is not paired with active learning. We believe that student engagement involves both a feeling about the learning, as well as completing effective learning practices based on that feeling. Engaged students take control of their own learning and make intentional decisions to ensure that they are successful learners. Please note that this definition was written by us, but it is based on a variety of literature on the topic of engagement. And we fully acknowledge that others may define the term "engagement" somewhat differently than we do.

With this in mind, we want to discuss this topic first, as good student engagement lays a foundation for all other learning in the online classroom. When it comes to student learning, especially in online courses, there are lots of myths out there! And we have found that the myths surrounding student engagement in learning are some of the most pervasive. Below, we do our best to debunk three of the top myths regarding student engagement in online courses.

The first myth we have encountered is that student engagement and motivation have no impact on learning, so worrying about them is a waste of time. The reality is that this belief is simply not true. Student engagement is a huge factor in student learning outcomes for all learners, preschool through college. When students are engaged in their learning, they have higher academic achievement in the course and better understanding of the learning material (Dierendonck et al., 2023; Ko et al., 2015). And when students enjoy the learning experience, they are more likely to attend class or participate in learning activities (Halm, 2015). Students who are more engaged in their learning also report higher levels of satisfaction with their learning experience (Marmolejo et al., 2004; Sun et al., 2024). Third, student engagement increases metacognitive awareness in the university classroom, including intentional focus on critical thinking skills (Dos & Eraslan, 2024). Finally, higher student satisfaction directly impacts student retention at the university (Eather et al., 2022; Schreiner, 2009), so faculty focus on engagement can have impacts beyond their own course.

Despite the fact that we know student engagement and motivation matter, the research (e.g., Pino-James, 2017) indicates that student engagement levels tend to be low. This indicates that engaging learners is vital and a critical focus area for all teachers, including online teacher educators. We must dedicate time and focus in our instructional planning to supporting students' engagement in our courses. In reality, Kathy and Marla probably spend more time on engagement-enhancing activities for their online courses than they spend on any other aspect of their courses. Student engagement simply matters that much to course success!

The second myth we commonly hear about student engagement is that university students choose to attend school (unlike PK–12 students), so they should have the intrinsic motivation to do what is required to ensure that they have successful learning experiences. According to Di Domenico and Ryan (2017), intrinsic motivation can be seen when people are self-determined to learn new skills, develop existing skills, and complete tasks in the absence of any external rewards for doing so.

The idea that intrinsic motivation is sufficient for ensuring student learning sounds great, but it does not really align with human nature. We, as teacher educators, often find ourselves unmotivated to do the things we need to do as parts of our jobs (in our chosen career path). For example, at the end of each semester, some of our colleagues create social media posts to share all the things they are doing instead of grading. The "because I should be grading" procrastination activities often include things such as cleaning the house, baking cookies, washing the car, weeding the garden, or going for a run. All of these things are productive, but in this case they are being used as a distraction from the task at hand. And we want to note here that all of our colleagues love their jobs and are fabulous teacher educators. But we can all feel discouragement and a lack of motivation, even for the things we love to do. We certainly cannot expect our students to feel motivated to learn 100% of the time if we don't feel motivated to do teaching tasks all the time!

In the classroom, we know that many factors impact students' intrinsic motivation for learning beyond simply their choice to enroll in the course. Student engagement and motivation in learning are impacted by a variety of factors outside our classrooms—at the university, community, national, and world levels (Oele et al., 2017). Student intrinsic motivation increases when students view the course content as relevant and useful (Moreno-Murcia et al., 2024). Student intrinsic motivation is also directly influenced by students' feelings of connectedness (Mueller & Schnurbus, 2023; Pelikan et al., 2021); we discuss this concept of building community in detail in Chapter 2. Student intrinsic motivation can also be impacted by various other factors, including (a) positive or negative interactions with their teacher (Bolkan et al., 2022), (b) experiencing cyberbullying from peers (Gulzar et al., 2022), and (c) the presence or absence of external rewards for success (Derfler-Rozin & Pitesa, 2020). Basically, what we know is that we cannot expect all students to be intrinsically motivated to learn at all times—it is simply not a realistic expectation. And the factors that have the most influence on intrinsic motivation for one student may not be the same factors that most influence another student's motivation. As teacher educators, we need to actively work to engage students in learning and help them stay motivated to succeed in our courses.

The final myth we would like to address regarding student engagement is that the same engagement strategies are effective for all learners. While many engagement strategies increase motivation and learning participation for the majority of learners, no strategy leads to the engagement of all learners, and teachers must utilize a variety of engagement strategies (Chakraborty & Nafukho, 2014; Pedler et al., 2020). Both university faculty and students believe that student engagement is important and that faculty must use a variety of engagement strategies (Bolliger & Martin, 2021). Factors such as student age, gender, and previous online learning experiences all impact students' levels of engagement and the strategies that support their learning engagement (Martin & Bolliger, 2018). It is also important to note that university faculty and their students are not in agreement regarding the importance of various engagement strategies, with faculty noting that various strategies are more vital for student success than students perceive them to be (Bolliger & Martin, 2018). This certainly does not mean that student engagement is not important—it just indicates that our students may not fully understand the value of our efforts to support their engagement.

Tools to Use—"I Do"

1 Offer Choice

In the book Introduction, we briefly introduced the concept of Universal Design for Learning (UDL), and we discuss this educational framework more thoroughly in Appendix D. The third principle of UDL is multiple means of action and expression, which indicates that we assess student knowledge using a variety of formats (Boothe et al., 2020). Offering choice is one of our favorite ways to incorporate the UDL principles into our online courses, as it supports the needs of all of our learners (plus, it can be a lot more fun to grade choice-based assignments, especially when you are teaching a large cohort of students!). Darling-Hammond et al. (2013) caution that effective assessment cannot occur when teachers rely solely on one form of assessing student learning; good assessment practices should include a variety of assessment tools.

One of the most common ways to offer student choice in the online classroom is through choice-based assignments in which students select how they want to demonstrate their own learning of the course or assignment objectives. Student learning can be accurately assessed through well-designed choice-based learning activities (Hanewicz et al., 2017; Jopp & Cohen, 2020). When faculty offer choices in the classroom, it impacts students' attitudes toward learning (Flowerday & Shell, 2015) and their willingness to do work beyond the minimum requirements (Hanewicz et al., 2017; Rideout, 2017).

We are definitely not saying that you have to allow students to have input into everything or always offer choices in your classroom. But when you offer students opportunities for choice and input, you are likely to find that your students will be better engaged throughout the course. When we offer students choices in their learning, either in the ways that they access information or in the ways they demonstrate their content mastery, we give them more ownership of their own learning. We help them to become "expert learners," which is a term used in the UDL literature (e.g., CAST, 2017; McDowell, 2018) to describe ideal learners.

We realize that not all students are good at writing or presenting and that many do not like to write papers or give presentations. Some students have strengths and talents in other areas—many of those talents will support their success in the PK–12 classroom, so we want to encourage their use of these skills in our programs. There are certainly times when students should not have a choice. If they need to write a lesson plan, they need to write it! An interpretive dance would not demonstrate their lesson plan writing skills! But there are times when any medium can be used to demonstrate student mastery of a learning concept. In those cases, we suggest (at least sometimes) offering choice.

There are a variety of methods for offering choice. Kathy has utilized a tic-tac-toe type activity where she lists specific activities, but the board also includes a free-choice activity where students can choose how to demonstrate their understanding of the content. Students will choose three activities in a row to complete. This allows the students to be creative and take more ownership of their learning. Past activities she has received from this project include a student writing and acting out a puppet play, writing a cookbook, and even writing a book of poems. From experience, she can tell you that these are a million percent more fun to grade!

The example found in Textbox 1.1 provides a choice activity where students choose a specific activity to complete to demonstrate their understanding of UDL. This can easily be adapted with different activities as well as content areas.

2 Vary Instructional Tools

A second strategy for supporting student engagement is the use of varied instructional tools. In our experience, many online faculty rely on textbook chapters and article readings as the primary forms of instruction in their courses. While having students read is one method of teaching, it cannot (and should not) be the only way that students are provided learning content in the course. When you use a variety of instructional tools in your classroom, you align your instruction with the UDL principle of multiple means of representation (CAST, 2024). We want to quickly remind you that good instruction often meets more than one UDL principle. When we use multiple means of representation in our courses, we also increase student engagement, which aligns with the UDL principle of multiple means of engagement.

By using varied instructional tools in your online course, you can work to reach the diverse needs and interests of your students. We want to quickly

> **Textbox 1.1**
>
> ## Universal Design for Learning Choice Activity
>
> Let's take the opportunity to practice what we are learning. Now it is your chance to choose how you want to deepen your understanding of UDL and how you want to demonstrate your understanding of UDL in the classroom. **You may choose one of the following assignments OR if you have another idea you may email me your idea, and if approved, you may complete that project.**
>
> **Professional Development Presentation:** Create a professional development presentation and record yourself presenting the information (either to an actual group or not). This should include interactions (e.g., discussions, activities, etc.) and cover any relevant information you determine other teachers need to be aware of regarding the topic of UDL. Your presentation should be approximately 20–30 minutes. When turning in your assignment, it is highly recommended that you submit a link to your recorded presentation (loading into Blackboard is NOT a good idea). Additionally, make sure to turn in your recording, your actual presentation (e.g., Prezi, PowerPoint, etc.), and your narrative (this needs to be done in a Word document and saved as a PDF).
>
> **Article Synopsis:** Locate a peer-reviewed article related to UDL from the library—do not use any that I provided in Canvas. Review your article and complete the Article Synopsis template form found HERE. There is also an example to help get your juices flowing.

note here that the idea of offering various methods for students to learn the content does not mean that we think students have learning styles. The concept of learning styles has been debunked in the literature (e.g., Ellis, 2024; Nancekivell et al., 2020; Whitman, 2023). Instead, we know that all students have learning preferences and that students tend to learn content better when it is presented to them in a variety of ways—students do best when they access the same information in multiple formats (Bresnahan et al., 2024). Recent research (Newton & Wang, 2024) indicates that learning preferences may be malleable and change over time, indicating that the same student may prefer accessing information differently from one course to the next or even from one week to the next.

Examples of different instructional tools can include having students read research articles, practitioner-based articles, blogs (that are credible and evidence based), government documents, or textbook chapters. You can also provide videos of the content in practice, give a live or recorded lecture, have students complete online modules, or incorporate student-led research and presentations. We both use many of these tools in our own online classrooms each week.

As an example, when Marla teaches students about the thirteen disability categories identified in federal law, she uses the materials listed below. Many of these materials provide the same information, which gives students the opportunity to see the learning material in a variety of formats. Students are expected to review each of these learning materials—there is not a choice to select the material(s) the student prefers. Over the years, Marla has learned that students better understand the disability categories and the distinctions between them because they receive the same basic information provided by a variety of experts in the field in various formats.

- Textbook chapter describing each disability category
- Individuals with Disabilities Education Improvement Act (IDEIA), Section 300.8, which is the precise wording for each disability category under federal law
- Colorado Department of Education disability categories webpage, which provides the definition for each category, as well as state-specific information about terminology and resources
- A video lecture she recorded describing each of the categories, including national- and state-level-specific information
- A video posted on YouTube by Understood.org that describes each of the categories

3 Schedule Announcements and Emails

A third strategy to engage learners in your online classroom is to intentionally plan and schedule course announcements at least a few times each week. These announcements can include both a video aspect and a written aspect to ensure the use of UDL principles. In these scheduled announcements, you can remind students of what they need to read for the module or even what is due for a particular module. This is also a great time to review assignment expectations or review items you caught from the previous module that students may need to work on for future assignments. You can also provide additional resources that may support student learning on course materials or share information about events and news in the field of education. By scheduling these announcements, students begin to depend on seeing them at specific times throughout the week, and it provides them a sort of check-in aspect to the course. In addition, we have found that sending these course announcements as emails in addition to posting them in the course increases student engagement. When students receive frequent emails from the instructor, they are reminded of the learning that is happening in the course and what they need to do to be successful.

The literature indicates that instructor presence in online courses increases student engagement and learning, as well as student satisfaction with the course (Ladyshewsky, 2013; Robertson et al., 2021). The use of strategies such as course announcements is a good, practical way to be present and visible in a course. We do, however, know that it might feel like just one more thing you need to do in your already busy day. We suspect that at least a few of you are reading this and thinking, "How can I do all of these things?" Remember that you should not try to do everything at once, and you should look for ways to use effective strategies while keeping your workload manageable. One of our favorite tips for announcements is to create a Word document for each course we teach and include the announcements for that course. The next time we teach the class, we can use the previous course announcements as a starting point for the current offering of the course. So, instead of writing new announcements a few times per week, we are just making small adjustments to previous work.

Kathy uses course announcements with her undergraduate courses most often. She has found that her undergraduate students do not usually attend the live virtual meetings—due to scheduling issues with their face-to-face classes—and thus she will post a lecture in the weekly content module; however, for the assignments, her students understand that an announcement will be posted at 6 a.m. on Mondays that includes any important notes for the week and areas to focus on. The announcement also includes a video in which she reviews the assignments and expectations. The final piece of the announcement is a written list of what is due that week and when, as well as a reminder that she is available during office hours and at other times as requested. Textbox 1.2 provides an example.

Marla posts course announcements (that she also sends as emails) every Monday, Wednesday, and Friday in each of her courses. The Monday announcements are overviews of the weekly expectations, including required readings and viewings, as well as a list of the assignments due that week. On Wednesdays and Fridays, she either shares additional optional resources related to the weekly learning or more specific information about assignments due that week (including sample assignments when appropriate). She also includes a funny meme, either related to the day of the week or to the course materials, at the bottom of each announcement, as she has found that this encourages students to read the entire announcement. In addition, when students tell her they never saw certain information, she can tell them to look at the announcement with the Monday Garfield meme (or something similar). Marla occasionally posts announcements on Tuesdays

---

Textbox 1.2

Announcement Example

Hello everyone!

The video below reviews the assignments that are due this week. Please make sure to review the video so you know the expectations for this week's assignment.

As a reminder—the following are due this week:

1 Chapter 6 Quiz

2 Week 9 Assignment (review early as there are interviews and observations for this week's assignment)

I hope you all have a great week, and if you have any questions, please reach out via email or sign up for a time to meet with me during my office hours. You can sign up for a time by clicking HERE!

—Dr. Boothe

and Thursdays when she notices students need additional clarification on something or simply need some words of encouragement.

4 Online Office Hours

A fourth recommendation for increasing learner engagement in your coursework is the use of online office hours. Creating weekly office hours via Zoom, InSpace, Google, etc. is an easy way to help meet the needs of your students, demonstrate your presence in the course, and support individual students. Students report that faculty who offer online office hours seem more available and accessible and demonstrate their commitment to student learning (Lohmann et al., 2018), and students prefer online office hours to traditional face-to-face office hours in the professor's office (Li & Pitts, 2009; Schauer et al., 2024).

In our experience, there are certain strategies that are vital for hosting successful office hours. First, you must explain to students what the term "office hours" means, as many students do not know. In fact, we have discovered that some students think the term means the hours in which we are unavailable because we are doing other work in our "office." Secondly, you must clearly communicate to students when and where you hold office hours. We suggest telling them at the beginning of the course, reminding them on occasion (such as in your weekly course announcements), and posting the information somewhere in the course. Third, and we know it may seem silly, but be available when you say you are going to be available. Pfund et al. (2013) found that about one-fourth of faculty were not in their office during face-to-face office hours. We suspect this number is similar, or even higher, for online office hours. Finally, because we know many online learners choose to take online courses due to other commitments in their lives, we need to ensure that we offer office hours at times that students may be able to meet with us. In reality, many online learners work full-time jobs and have families, so they may be unavailable during the traditional 8–5 workday. We suggest that you plan at least one weekly office hour on an evening or weekend.

Kathy has held virtual office hours several different ways. In some courses, she is available during her office hours for anyone to show up, no appointment needed. At other times she has specific hours available for office hours, but she has her students use her Calendly link to sign up for times. This ensured that she was aware they would be there and helped remind the student when to be online for the meeting.

Marla hosts a weekly office hour (which is really only thirty minutes) for each class she teaches. Students with questions about course content or assignments are encouraged to attend these sessions. Marla has found that many students without questions attend these class office hours to hear what others are asking, making this strategy an easy way to answer questions in an expedited manner. In addition, she offers individual office hours by appointment using her Calendly link, which links directly to her work calendar and offers both daytime and evening availability.

5 Group Work

Another option for supporting online student engagement is the use of group work. When students have the opportunity to learn collaboratively through group activities, their engagement in learning may be increased (Ainsworth, 2021; VanRyzin et al. 2020). Students report that online group work is most effective when clear guidelines and expectations are provided by the course instructor and group communication norms are proactively established at the onset of the work (Hill, 2023). Throughout the group work and at the culmination of the work, it is important that students have the opportunity to evaluate their own participation in the group and the work of their classmates (Adesina et al., 2023; Weaver & Esposto, 2012). Group activities in the online classroom are endless but may include small-group or partner assignments or projects or asynchronous discussion groups.

An example of a collaborative learning project that Kathy has used (and loved) is a book study. Students chose a book they wanted to read that was written by a person with autism. They then signed up for a group to work with. If they knew other students in the class, they could choose to work with those classmates. If they did not have friends in the class, they created "draft cards" where they put information on their available hours, their contact information, their collaboration preferences, and other information they wanted to share with potential project teammates. (Kathy wants to note that she got this idea from another fabulous education professor.) Students read these draft cards and reached out to students with similar work schedules or work ethics to create a group. Once groups were established, they were given directions on the project, a sample timeline, and a group member grading form. At the end of the project, students completed the group member grading form independently.

Marla has used small-group asynchronous discussions, especially in some of her larger courses. Generally she has all students participate in the same discussion thread. But occasionally, especially when the class is larger or for courses that include students from various degree paths, she uses assigned discussion groups. Marla chooses group assignments based on the purpose of the discussion. Sometimes the groups are random, and other times she creates groups based on the career goals (or current teaching positions) of students. Sometimes she puts together groups of students with similar teaching positions/career goals, and sometimes the groups intentionally include students from a variety of teaching positions so they can better understand the perspectives of teachers (this is especially useful for courses that include both general and special educators or elementary and secondary teachers). When assigning these groups, she sends an email to students telling them their assigned group and puts the last name of each group member in the discussion thread title—this helps students quickly identify their assigned group. Students are encouraged to look at the discussions other groups are having (and contribute when appropriate), but are only required to actively participate in their assigned group.

6 Flipped Classroom

The final engagement activity we would like to share in this chapter is the use of the flipped classroom model. This strategy is ideal for online courses that include a synchronous component. The flipped classroom model is appropriate when the initial teaching of content occurs in an asynchronous format and follow-up activities are completed synchronously (Bintz et al., 2024). The use of a flipped classroom increases student interactions with one another and with the course instructor during synchronous learning, leading to increased engagement in instruction (Çelik et al., 2021; Faro et al., 2024). In addition, students who consistently complete the asynchronous course components, including viewing prerecorded lectures, participate more fully in the synchronous class sessions and demonstrate increased mastery of course content (Lin et al., 2019) and an increase in their critical thinking skills within the course content area (Orhan, 2023).

Marla uses the flipped classroom model in the alternative licensure program she directs. Before she began overseeing the program, the course met via Zoom for two hours every other week, with a different learning topic for each class session. The first hour of class was spent with the instructor giving a lecture on the topic before moving into about an hour of class activities based on the lecture topic. Each section of the course received a lecture from their instructor, meaning different sections of the course received different information on the topic. Between class sessions, students completed follow-up activities based on the lectures and read one or two textbook chapters each week. When students provided end-of-course feedback, several students noted the challenges associated with long synchronous class sessions as a first-year teacher who is busy with lesson planning, grading, and meeting school requirements. In addition, several students noted that they worked in schools with other students in the program who were in different sections of the class—when they talked about the course, they discovered they were learning different (and sometimes conflicting) information. Based on the student feedback and her knowledge of the benefits of the flipped classroom model, Marla decided to change the course to meet for only an hour. All the lectures are prerecorded by her and embedded in the courses; students are expected to view the lectures and complete other learning tasks on the weeks when class does not meet. Then, during the shorter class sessions, students engage in class activities and discussions related to the topic, building on what they heard in the lecture. Student feedback on the new course design has been positive, leading Marla to surmise that the flipped classroom model is working well for her alternative licensure students.

Assessing Your Own Teaching Tools

In this chapter, we have offered six ideas for increasing learner engagement in your online courses: (a) offering choice, (b) varying instructional tools, (c) scheduling course announcements, (d) hosting online office hours, (e) the use of group work, and (f) the flipped classroom model. Keep in mind that these six recommendations are simply that—recommendations. We have in no way provided a comprehensive list of engagement strategies for your online courses. We are simply sharing a few of our favorite teaching strategies. In reality, we could probably write an entire book on engaging online learners

Table 1.1 Tools for Supporting Student Engagement in Online Learning

Name	Link
ScreenPal (video editing)	https://screenpal.com
IRIS Center (learning modules)	https://iris.peabody.vanderbilt.edu
Center for Assessment (learning modules)	https://www.nciea.org/library/classroom-assessment-learning-modules/
Microsoft (scheduled emails)	https://support.microsoft.com/en-us/office/delay-or-schedule-sending-email-messages-in-outlook-026af69f-c287-490a-a72f-6c65793744ba
Canva (meme generator)	https://www.canva.com/create/memes/
ImgFlip (meme generator)	https://imgflip.com/memegenerator/27596988/Free
Zoom (scheduler)	https://www.zoom.com/en/products/appointment-scheduler
Calendly (scheduler)	https://calendly.com
Doodle Polls (scheduler)	https://doodle.com/en/product/polls/

in teacher education courses (and because it really is one of our favorite topics, we might do that one day!). There are so many amazing strategies and ideas for supporting the engagement and motivation of the students in your classroom. Table 1.1 offers our (limited) recommendations for tools that faculty may use to support student engagement in the online classroom.

Avoid This

While it is important to know what to do to engage learners, it is also important that we share with you some things to avoid. This is similar to telling our students that sometimes you learn more from watching teachers do the wrong thing than you do watching a "perfect" teacher. The following is a list of items we have personally done or seen/heard other instructors do that they have learned is not all that effective.

1 Focusing on student engagement and motivation at the expense of student learning

In this chapter, we have emphasized the importance of student engagement. It matters immensely and is a vital way to spend our time as online teacher educators. However, it is not the only thing we need to do in our classrooms. Spend time putting effective engagement practices in your course. Check course analytics to determine how frequently, and for how long, students are actively engaging in the course shell. But do more than this. Make sure that you are teaching the content your course aims to teach. Complete your other job requirements (service, research, writing, mentoring, and answering endless emails). Take care of yourself and your family. Focus on your own professional development—read articles and talk to other scholars. Doing all of these things, and demonstrating to your students that teaching is important and good teaching multifaceted, will make you more effective in the classroom and better prepare your students for their PK–12 teaching careers.

2 Relying on the strategies that support your own engagement without considering the diverse needs and motivations of your students

As teachers, we often instinctively default to the teaching strategies that worked best for us as students. This holds true for the engagement strategies we tend to rely on in our online courses. But we have to remember that our learning preferences are not necessarily the same learning preferences that our students exhibit. With this in mind, we must utilize various engagement strategies and tools, even if they don't align with our preferences. Marla strongly dislikes group work and (almost always) wants to work alone. When she first started teaching online, she refused to do any group activities. But students began to request it, so she looked for opportunities to include these in her courses. Student feedback indicates that doing so was the right choice, despite her personal dislike for the strategy.

3 Expecting students to be engaged and motivated 100% of the time

As we noted earlier in the chapter, nobody is focused and engaged all the time. That is simply not realistic. We would venture to guess that while reading this chapter, you lost focus more than once. Maybe a student entered your office, or your child's school called to say your son is sick and you need to pick him up, or an email arrived in your inbox and you stopped reading to check your email. And, if we are totally honest, we lost focus countless times while writing and editing this chapter. You have chosen to read this book, and we chose to write it. But we have other priorities and responsibilities in our lives. So do our students. There will be times when your students are worried about their mother's failing health or how they will pay rent that month—those worries will interrupt their learning. Your students may be hungry, tired, or simply completely overwhelmed. While they have chosen to take your course and do want to learn the content, they will not be 100% engaged at all times. When this happens, don't blame yourself and don't blame your students. Aim for students who are engaged most of the time and are demonstrating mastery of course learning materials.

Let's Practice—"We Do"

Professor Laurent is teaching a Philosophy of Education course that includes both synchronous and asynchronous components. The course meets for ninety minutes every Wednesday evening. The students taking the course are all pursuing graduate degrees in curriculum and instruction and have all been teachers for a minimum of five years, but they teach in a variety of grades and content areas and are located all over the state. After the first few weeks of the course, Professor Laurent has noticed that many students keep their cameras off during synchronous class sessions and never respond when questions are asked nor participate in class discussions or activities. Professor Laurent would like to add some engagement strategies to his course to support student participation, motivation, and learning.

Now it is time to practice. This is the "We Do" part of good teaching. Answer the questions in Textbox 1.3 using the blank spaces provided. Once you have your answers, compare them with our answers in Appendix A and share your thoughts on social media using the hashtag #OnlineTeacherPrep and tagging us.

Textbox 1.3

1. In your experience, why might Professor Laurent's students not be participating in the course?

2. What immediate action can Professor Laurent take to enhance student engagement in the course? What can he do today?

3. What three strategies should Professor Laurent implement over the next month? What action steps does he need to take in order to implement those strategies?

4. As Professor Laurent prepares to teach this same course again next semester, what should he be considering?

5. What are the top 5 tips you have for Professor Laurent regarding student engagement in his course?

Apply to Your Own Courses—"You Do"

It is now your time to practice engaging learners in your own online course. Follow the steps in Textbox 1.4 to proactively increase student engagement, motivation, and learning.

Textbox 1.4

1 Identify a course you teach in which student engagement is often low (or lower than you would prefer).

2 Now choose one strategy discussed in this chapter that you would like to implement in your online classroom. Be sure the strategy you select is realistic within your limitations (time, resources, etc.).

3 Once the course is identified and you have a chosen strategy, open your course learning management system (LMS) and look for a place to start. You may consider looking at the analytics collected by the LMS, which will give you insight into the specific assignments or course materials with which students engage for longer periods of time and those in which they minimally engage (or don't engage at all).

(Continued)

> **Textbox 1.4 (Continued)**
>
> 4 The hard part is done—now you get to implement the strategy—this is the fun part! Develop your strategy and insert it into the appropriate place in your LMS.
>
> **Congratulations!**—You have started the process of increasing student engagement in your online class! Now try it again for another course or add another strategy to this course.

References

Adesina, O. O., Adesina, O. A., Adelopo, I., & Afrifa, G. A. (2023). Managing group work: The impact of peer assessment on student engagement. *Accounting Education, 32*(1), 90–113. https://doi.org/10.1080/09639284.2022.2034023

Ainsworth, J. (2021). Team-based learning in professional writing courses for accounting graduates: Positive impacts on student engagement, accountability and satisfaction. *Accounting Education, 30*(3), 234–257. https://doi.org/10.1080/09639284.2021.1906720

Bintz, G., Barenberg, J., & Dutke, S. (2024). Components of the flipped classroom in higher education: Disentangling flipping and enrichment. *Frontiers in Education, 9.* https://doi.org/10.3389/feduc.2024.1412683

Bolkan, S., Goodboy, A. K., Shin, M., & Chiasson, R. M. (2022). Teacher antagonism: Reducing students' sustained attention through decreased affect toward instructors and diminished motivation to learn. *Communication Education, 71*(3), 188–203. https://doi.org/10.1080/03634523.2022.2070771

Bolliger, D. U., & Martin, F. (2018). Instructor and student perceptions of online student engagement strategies. *Distance Education, 39*(4), 568–583. https://doi.org/10.1080/01587919.2018.1520041

Bolliger, D. U., & Martin, F. (2021). Factors underlying the perceived importance of online student engagement strategies. *Journal of Applied Research in Higher Education, 13*(2), 404–419. https://doi.org/10.1108/JARHE-02-2020-0045

Boothe, K. A., Lohmann, M. J., & Owiny, R. L. (2020). Enhancing student learning in the online instructional environment through the use of Universal Design for Learning. *Networks: An Online Journal for Teacher Research, 22*(1). https://doi.org/10.4148/2470-6353.1310

Bresnahan, C., Grossnickle Peterson, E., & Hattan, C. (2024). Why educators endorse a neuromyth: Relationships among educational priorities, beliefs about learning styles, and instructional decisions. *Frontiers in Psychology, 15*. https://doi.org/10.3389/fpsyg.2024.1407518

CAST. (2017). *UDL tips for fostering expert learners*. https://www.cast.org/products-services/resources/2017/udl-tips-fostering-expert-learners

CAST. (2024). *Universal Design for Learning guidelines* (Version 3.0). https://udlguidelines.cast.org

Çelik, H., Pektas, H. M., & Karamustafaoglu, O. (2021). The effects of the flipped classroom model on the laboratory self-efficacy and attitude of higher education students. *Electronic Journal for Research in Science & Mathematics Education, 25*(2), 47–67.

Chakraborty, M., & Nafukho, M. (2014). Strengthening student engagement: What do students want in online courses? *European Journal of Training and Development, 38*(9), 782–802. https://doi.org/10.1108/EJTD-11-2013-0123.

Darling-Hammond, L., Herman, J., Pellegrino, J., Abedi, J., Aber, J. L., Baker, E., Bennett, R., Gordon, E., Haertel, E., Hakuta, K., Ho, A., Linn, R. L., Pearson, P. D., Popham, J., Resnick, L., Schoenfield, A. H., Shavelson, R., Shepard, L. A., Shulman, L., & Steele, C. M. (2013). *Criteria for high-quality assessment*. Stanford Center for Opportunity Policy in Education.

Derfler-Rozin, R., & Pitesa, M. (2020). Motivation purity bias: Expression of extrinsic motivation undermines perceived intrinsic motivation and engenders bias in selection decisions. *Academy of Management Journal, 63*(6), 1840–1864. https://doi.org/10.5465/amj.2017.0617

Di Domenico, S. I., & Ryan, R. M. (2017). The emerging neuroscience of intrinsic motivation: A new frontier in self-determination research. *Frontiers in Human Neuroscience, 11*, 145. https://doi.org/10.3389/fnhum.2017.00145

Dierendonck, C., Tóth-Király, I., Morin, A. J. S., Kerger, S., Milmeister, P., & Poncelet, D. (2023). Testing associations between global and specific levels of student academic motivation and engagement in the classroom. *Journal of Experimental Education, 91*(1), 101–124. https://doi.org/10.1080/00220973.2021.1913979

Dös, B., & Eraslan, A. (2024). Investigating the relationship between university students' classroom engagement and metacognitive awareness. *Journal on Educational Psychology, 17*(4), 13–25.

Eather, N., Mavilidi, M. F., Sharp, H., & Parkes, R. (2022). Programmes targeting student retention/success and satisfaction/experience in higher education: A systematic review. *Journal of Higher Education Policy and Management, 44*(3), 223–239. https://doi.org/10.1080/1360080X.2021.2021600

Ellis, E. (2024). Education is still failing students by pedalling debunked learning styles. *Education Journal Review, 29*(3), 144–147.

Faro, M. H., Gutu, T. S., & Hunde, A. B. (2024). Improving student engagement with a flipped classroom instruction model in Ethiopian higher education institutions: The case of Mattu University. *PLOS One, 19*(10), 1–17. https://doi.org/10.1371/journal.pone.0307382

Flowerday, T., & Shell, D. F. (2015). Disentangling the effects of interest and choice on learning, engagement, and attitude. *Learning and Individual Differences, 40*, 134–140. https://doi.org/10.1016/j.lindif.2015.05.003

Gulzar, M. A., Ahmad, M., Hassan, M., & Rasheed, M. I. (2022). How social media use is related to student engagement and creativity: Investigating through the lens of intrinsic motivation. *Behaviour & Information Technology, 41*(11), 2283–2293. https://doi.org/10.1080/0144929X.2021.1917660

Halm, D. S. (2015). The impact of engagement on student learning. *International Journal of Education and Social Science, 2*(2), 22–33.

Hanewicz, C., Platt, A., & Arendt, A. (2017). Creating a learner-centered teaching environment using student choice in assignments. *Distance Education, 38*(3), 273–287. https://doi.org/10.1080/01587919.2017.1369349

Hill, C., Abu-Ayyash, E., & Charles, T. (2023). By nature, a social animal: An exploration of perceptions of online group work. *Cambridge Journal of Education, 53*(5), 665–681. https://doi.org/10.1080/0305764X.2023.2206795

Jopp, R., & Cohen, J. (2020). Choose your own assessment—Assessment choice for students in online higher education. *Teaching in Higher Education, 27*(6), 738–755. https://doi.org/10.1080/13562517.2020.1742680

Ko, J. W., Park, S., Yu, H. S., Kim, S.-J., & Kim, D. M. (2015). The structural relationship between student engagement and learning outcomes in Korea. *The Asia-Pacific Education Researcher, 25*, 147–157. https://doi.org/10.1007/s40299-015-0245-2

Ladyshewsky, R. K. (2013). Instructor presence in online courses and student satisfaction. *International Journal for the Scholarship of Teaching and Learning, 7*(1), Article 13.

Li, L., & Pitts, J. P. (2009). Does it really matter? Using virtual office hours to enhance student-faculty interaction. *Journal of Information Systems Education, 20*(2), 175–185.

Lin, L. C., Hung, I. C., Kinshuk, & Chen, N. S. (2019). The impact of student engagement on learning outcomes in a cyber-flipped classroom. *Educational Technology Research and Development, 67*, 1573–1591. https://doi.org/10.1007/s11423-019-09698-9

Lohmann, M. J., Boothe, K. A., Hathcote, A. R., & Turpin, A. (2018). Engaging graduate students in the online learning environment: A Universal Design for Learning (UDL) approach to teacher preparation. *Networks: An Online Journal for Teacher Research, 20*(2), Article 5. https://doi.org/10.4148/2470-6353.1264

Mann, S., & Robinson, A. (2009). Boredom in the lecture theatre: An investigation into the contributors, moderators and outcomes of boredom amongst university students. *British Educational Research Journal, 35*(2), 243–258.

Marmolejo, E. K., Wilder, D. A., & Bradley, L. (2004). A preliminary analysis of the effects of response cards on student performance and participation in an upper division university course. *Journal of Applied Behavior Analysis, 37*, 405–410.

Martin, F., & Bolliger, D. U. (2018). Engagement matters: Student perceptions on the importance of engagement strategies in the online learning environment. *Online Learning, 22*(1), 205–222.

McDowell, M. (2018). *Developing expert learners: A roadmap for growing confident and competent students.* Sage Publishing.

Moreno-Murcia, J. A., Huéscar Hernández, E., León, J., Fin, G., Nodari Júnior, R. J., Valero-Valenzuela, A., Tristan, J., Gastélum-Cuadras, G., Zueck Enríquez, M. del C., Vargas Vitoria, R., Cid, L., Monteiro, D., & Teixeira, D. (2024). Motivation to learn: An international multilevel study on student autonomy and teacher emphasis on content usefulness. *Anales de Psicología, 40*(2), 265–271. https://doi.org./10.6018/analesps.571161

Mueller, E. F., & Schnurbus, J. (2023). Heeding the call of science: What leads PhD graduates to pursue an academic career? *Academy of Management Learning & Education, 22*(4), 681–701. https://doi.org/10.5465/amle.2021.0216

Nancekivell, S. E., Shah, P., & Gelman, S. A. (2020). Maybe they're born with it, maybe it's experience: Towards a deeper understanding of the learning style myth. *Journal of Educational Psychology, 112*(2), 221–235. http://dx.doi.org/10.1037/edu0000366

Newton, S., & Wang, R. (2024). What the malleability of Kolb's learning style preferences reveals about categorical difference in learning. *Educational Studies, 50*(5), 1014–1033. https://doi.org/10/1080/03055698.2021.2025044

Oele, M., DiGiammarino, P., Keiffer, M. R., LaVigne, M. R., Nicely, M. V., & Nosek, M. (2017). Examining assumptions about student engagement in the classroom: A faculty learning community's yearlong journey. *Jesuit Higher Education: A Journal, 6*(1), Article 14. https://epublications.regis.edu/jhe/vol6/iss1/14

Orhan, A. (2023). Comparing the effectiveness of online, flipped, and in-class critical thinking instruction on critical thinking skills and dispositions in higher education: Flipped classroom produces the greatest gains. *International Journal of Technology in Education, 6*(2), 238–259.

Pedler, M., Hudson, S., & Yeigh, T. (2020). The teachers' role in student engagement: A review. *Australian Journal of Teacher Education, 45*(3), 48–62.

Pelikan, E. R., Korlat, S., Reiter, J., Holzer, J., Mayerhofer, M., Schober, B., Spiel, C., Hamzallari, O., Uka, A., Chen, J., Välimäki, M., Puharić, Z., Anusionwu, K. E., Okocha, A. N., Zabrodskaja, A., Salmela-Aro, K., Käser, U., Schultze-Krumbholz, A., Wachs, S.,... Lüftenegger, M. (2021). Distance learning in higher education during COVID-19: The role of basic psychological needs and intrinsic motivation for persistence and procrastination—A multi-country study. *PLOS One, 16*(10). https://doi.org/10.1371/journal.pone.0257346

Pfund, R. A., Rogan, J. D., Burnham, B. R., & Norcross, J. C. (2013). Is the professor in? Faculty presence during office hours. *College Student Journal, 47*(3), 524–528.

Pino-James, N. (2017). Evaluation of a pedagogical model for student engagement in learning activities. *Educational Action Research, 26*(3), 456–479. https://doi.org/10.1080/09650792.2017.1354771

Rideout, C. A. (2017). Students' choices and achievement in large undergraduate classes using a novel flexible assessment approach. *Assessment & Evaluation in Higher Education, 43*(1), 68–78. https://doi.org/10.1080/02602938.2017.1294144

Robertson, S. N., Steele, J. P., & Mandernach, B. J. (2021). Exploring value variations in instructor presence techniques for online students. *InSight: A Journal of Scholarly Teaching, 16*, 16–49.

Schauer, S., Pakala, K., & Bairaktarova, D. (2024). Virtual "happy" office hours: The student experience. *Advances in Engineering Education, 12*(1), 3–24.

Schreiner, L. A. (2009). *Linking student satisfaction and retention*. Noel-Levitz. https://learn.ruffalonl.com/rs/395-EOG-977/images/LinkingStudentSatis0809.pdf

Sun, Q., Ackerman, D. S., & Fu, N. (2024). Student engagement and class satisfaction in an undergraduate marketing course: A 5-year longitudinal study. *Marketing Education Review, 34*(3), 175–186.

Van Ryzin, M. J., Roseth, C. J., & McClure, H. (2020). The effects of cooperative learning on peer relations, academic support, and engagement in learning among students of color. *Journal of Educational Research, 113*(4), 283–291. https://doi.org/10.1080/00220671.2020.1806016

Weaver, D., & Esposto, A. (2012). Peer assessment as a method of improving student engagement. *Assessment & Evaluation in Higher Education, 37*(7), 805–816. https://doi.org/10.1080/02602938.2011.576309

Whitman, G. M. (2023). Learning styles: Lack of research-based evidence. *Clearing House, 96*(4), 111–115. https://doi.org/10.1080/00098655.2023.2203891

2 Building Online Learning Communities

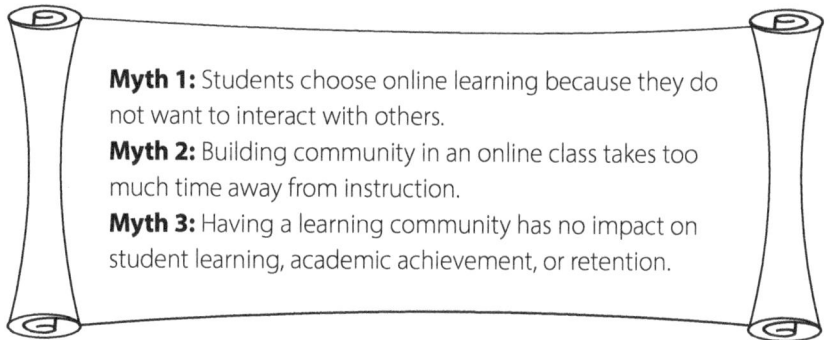

Myth 1: Students choose online learning because they do not want to interact with others.
Myth 2: Building community in an online class takes too much time away from instruction.
Myth 3: Having a learning community has no impact on student learning, academic achievement, or retention.

Debunking the Myths

There are several myths about the role of community building in learning, and the list above offers just a few of these. We have both heard from many colleagues the false belief that students frequently choose to take online courses because they do not want to interact with others. There is a belief that online learners have selected this medium of instruction because they prefer to learn alone. In reality, students tend to choose online learning for a variety of reasons, including (a) the flexibility inherent in online learning (Keis et al., 2017), (b) work or family commitments that make attending face-to-face courses challenging (Stone et al., 2016), and (c) not living near a university that offers the student's desired degree (Harris & Martin, 2012). In addition, the research indicates that many online learners seek a learning community within their courses (Berry, 2019) and perceive their own learning to be enhanced through a community (Liu et al., 2007). In our experience, each of these facts is very true. Our students regularly tell us that they appreciate online learning because it allows them to meet the many commitments in their lives while pursuing a degree, but that they also enjoy building relationships with their classmates and their professors. Clearly, having a learning community is an important aspect of learning, whether that learning occurs in a face-to-face or online classroom.

A second myth that we often hear is that faculty are not responsible for creating a learning community and that doing so will take time away from learning. We adamantly disagree with this belief. The reality is that an online learning community is primarily created through the efforts of faculty (Bolliger & Halupa, 2012), and the ways in which we design our courses and our active participation in the course can help to create a sense of community among students (Berry, 2019). In our experience, building a learning community in our courses does take some time, but no more time than building community in a face-to-face course.

The final myth about online learning communities we want to address is the belief that students do not benefit from being in a community. There is significant research to debunk this myth. Feeling a sense of community in a course leads to numerous benefits for learners, including (a) retention in the course and the academic program (Jacobs & Archie, 2008), (b) reduced levels of stress (Benson & Whitson, 2022), (c) student engagement in learning (Pike et al., 2011), and (d) a feeling of belonging and trust among learners (Berry, 2019; Bolliger & Halupa., 2019). As university faculty members, we have experienced all of these benefits in our students. And during the COVID pandemic, we personally witnessed the ways in which a learning community aided our students in managing both school-related and life stresses.

Many online learners feel isolated, alone, and like they are lost or disconnected from their school, instructor, and other students (Huang, 2002; McInnerney & Roberts, 2004; Paxton, 2003; Splitter, 2009). This strongly impacts how students perform in our classes, which makes it necessary for us to find ways to build community. This chapter will provide you with ideas on ways to build community that you can implement in your online classroom immediately. We have personally done many of these in our classes to build community among students and between students and ourselves. There is also a list of resources that can be used to help get you started with building community in your online course(s).

Tools to Use—"I Do"

As discussed earlier in this chapter, community is an important element that should be incorporated into all online courses. The following ideas are real-life examples of how you can incorporate community building into your online course(s). The goal of providing these examples is to open your mind to the possibilities that can be accomplished in the online classroom and begin sparking ideas on how you can make them your own. As you read the remainder of the chapter, identify ways you can make these ideas work for you and your courses' specific needs. Then feel free to share on social media and with your colleagues so that we can continue to build our online teaching toolboxes. Please remember to use the hashtag #OnlineTeacherPrep and tag both of us in your post.

1 Icebreakers/Polls

According to Berry (2019), providing a "Getting to Know You" area facilitated by the instructor is an effective and easy way to build community in your classroom. Two ways to create areas for students to get to know one another and their instructor are to create icebreakers and/or polls, which are fairly easy to incorporate into the online classroom. The use of an icebreaker can help students feel confident knowing they are valued in the group and their input will be heard and respected (Knickle & McNaughton, 2021). Faculty can use icebreakers and polls both with synchronous and asynchronous classes.

If you are hosting weekly virtual meetings, you can post a poll in which students come into the meeting and, while waiting for the meeting to begin, can answer a variety of questions that you can discuss during the first few minutes of class. You can do the same thing with an icebreaker, where you pose a question and students use the whiteboard feature in Zoom, or where students go and find an object and bring it to the meeting. You can then discuss this prompt and have students share in a large group or in breakout groups. The poll example in Textbox 2.1 demonstrates the kinds of questions that can be posed—easily manipulated for your specific purposes—to the class on the first night of class to spark a discussion. This can help students get to know one another and provide a valuable resource—other students—that can help them throughout the course and/or program.

Textbox 2.1

Poll Questions

1 How many previous courses have you taken with me?
   a This is my first course with you!

   b 1–2

   c 3–5

   d This is my last course with you!

2 How far into the program are you?
   a This is my first course and I am really nervous!

   b This is my first course and I am not at all nervous! I got this!

   c I have had 1–4 courses and I get more confident by the course!

   d I have had 5–9 courses and I think I've just about got it all figured out!

   e This is it! I am ready to be done and graduate!

3 What is your major?
   a Special Education

   b General Education

   c Educational Administration

   d Curriculum and Instruction

   e Something else!

4 If you teach, what do you teach?
   a Elementary special education

   b Elementary general education

   c Secondary special education

   d Secondary general education

   e I am not a teacher.

For asynchronous courses, you can also use both icebreakers and polls. They will just look a little different and may incorporate some of the ideas and tools discussed later in this chapter. The polls used in asynchronous online courses may consist of a Poll Everywhere survey that you post on Monday morning and ask a question related to strategies associated with the week's content. You would give your students one to two days to answer, and then you could post the results or create a short—less than one minute—video about the results. Asynchronous icebreakers can be used in many different ways—students can post short video clips, they can take pictures and include a short written piece, they can post a written thread, etc. The examples in Textboxes 2.2 and 2.3 can be used to help the instructor and students get to know each other.

Textbox 2.2

Icebreaker Activity #1

In the discussion thread labeled Icebreaker #1, do the following:

1. Find something in your house that represents your teaching. Take a picture of this and post to the discussion thread.

2. In your discussion thread, also create a 30-second video where you record yourself holding your item and tell your classmates how this item represents your teaching.

3. For fun, respond to other classmates with how you think the item represents teaching. Watch the video and then check to see if you were right!

Textbox 2.3

Icebreaker Activity #2

In the discussion thread labeled Icebreaker #2 do the following:

1. Take a "Back to School" photo of yourself.

2. In your photo or separately, list your favorite things. I have included a sample in the discussion thread.

2 Question & Answer Board

Supporting online learners through the use of interactive communication tools is another effective way to build community (Lohmann et al., 2018; McInnerney & Roberts, 2004). One way to do this is to provide a question-and-answer discussion board as an informal way for students to engage with classmates and faculty (Boothe et al., 2018). The question-and-answer discussion board is a discussion board where students go to ask general questions about assignments and other course-related questions. This would be best done using the discussion thread function in your school's learning management system (LMS). Faculty can also use this as a way to communicate and update assignment requirements. The instructor should check this daily and also remind students to check it often. Additionally, the instructor does not have to be the only person to answer questions. Having students take on the role of answering questions in the discussion board is an effective way to help students feel included and as though they are helping (a common motivation for teacher educators), and it also can help other students get answers more quickly (Jackson, 2019).

Kathy has found that students who have had her for a few classes often know a bit more about her, her grading style, and her expectations, so they are able to answer questions for other students, which is helpful for all those students working late at night, when the instructor is not! Having the question-and-answer discussion board also cuts back on the number of emails an instructor has to respond to with the same information. An example of the discussion prompt our university provided to faculty can be found in Textbox 2.4.

Textbox 2.4

Q & A Discussion Prompt

Got questions? Use this space to ask general course-related questions!

Please review this board frequently to see if clarification has been provided that you wouldn't want to miss!

3 Student Lounge

A student lounge is an informal discussion board where students can talk to each other about their coursework, other courses, or personal information such as jobs, families, and hobbies. This discussion board may or may not be monitored by the faculty and can be used in conjunction with the question-and-answer discussion board discussed above. The student lounge would be similar to MeetUp, which is an app where students come together to discuss their courses, and possibly even their professors! Student lounges can be created in your LMS with the discussion thread option, or you can create these in any web-based program you find (see Table 2.1 on p. 49 for some ideas). The prompt in Textbox 2.5 can be used as an introduction to the discussion board.

4 Social Media

Another option for building community in an online course is the use of social media. Bosch (2009) reports that social media can support student learning and create educational micro-communities, which are defined as groups with specialized learning and knowledge within a larger learning community (Ervin-Kassab & Drouin, 2021). Similarly, Abdelmalak (2015) and Lohmann et al. (2018) report that the use of Twitter can support community building.

Textbox 2.5

Student Lounge Prompt

This is your space, and I will not be monitoring conversations unless it is brought to my attention that inappropriate discussions are occurring. Use this as a place to get advice on coursework, upcoming courses, or even to solicit ideas or advice on how to best work with your students. In addition, use this space to talk about hobbies and families. This is your space—use it as you need! Please ensure that all comments are respectful and honor confidentiality.

We both use social media in a variety of ways to support our current and former students. Marla is a huge fan of Twitter/X and uses it as a tool for her own professional development, as well as for online teaching. She tweets resources for student use and hosts Twitter chats, which allow her students to interact with one another, program graduates, and professionals in the field of education. When using Twitter chats, it is important to create hashtags for the chats and teach students how to use those hashtags and how to reply to one another. Appropriate hashtags might include the course number or name and something related to the topic being discussed. Marla has also created a hashtag for her program (#CCUSPED), and she uses it when tweeting information or resources for her students. At the conclusion of a Twitter chat, she assembles the tweets into a PDF and posts it in her course—this allows all students to access the conversation, even if they are not Twitter users. Textbox 2.6 shows a sample Twitter chat that an education professor might use. You will notice that this figure, like a real chat, may include participation from anyone on Twitter and may not be sequential.

In addition to hosting her own Twitter chats, Marla highly encourages students to participate in Twitter chats hosted by others and to tweet about the things they are learning. In her experience, the use of Twitter can help online learners build a sense of community with their classmates, their professors, and other educators around the world.

Textbox 2.6

Sample Excerpt of Twitter Chat

Marla Lohmann: @MarlaLohmann

We are currently learning about the Universal Design for Learning (UDL) framework. UDL helps to reduce the barriers that are inherent in learning. Think about being an online learner—what barriers do you face? #CCUSPED #SED500 #UDL

Textbox 2.6 (Continued)

Student 1: @PretendStudent

@MarlaLohmann. I sometimes feel alone when I take online classes. I want to feel connected to my classmates and my professors. #CCUSPED #SED500 #UDL

Student 2: @AnotherPretendStudent

@PretendStudent. Me too! I want to be able to talk to my classmates and see people's faces. #CCUSPED #SED500 #UDL

Marla Lohmann: @MarlaLohmann

Great point, @PretendStudent and @AnotherPretendStudent. The independence and social isolation can be a barrier to online learning. How can teachers address this and help reduce or remove this barrier? #CCUSPED #SED500 #UDL

Education Professor: @Education Professor

@MarlaLohmann. Thanks for hosting this chat. I am not in your class, but I believe that one way we reduce this barrier is through intentional community building and doing things like hosting Twitter chats. #CCUSPED #SED500 #UDL

Student 2: @AnotherPretendStudent

@Education Professor. I agree! That is why I always attend these chats. I love to talk to my classmates in real time. #CCUSPED #SED500 #UDL

ProgramGraduate: @ProgramGraduate

@AnotherPretendStudent. Keep attending these, even when you graduate! I finished the program two years ago, but still feel so connected to #CCUSPED and the field because I get to tweet with everyone! #SED500 #UDL

Kathy uses Facebook to build community among graduates from her program. She has created a private Facebook group and invites all students to join upon graduation. Members of this group can share resources, ask questions, or just provide support to one another. Marla created a similar Facebook group but has not seen students using it consistently. Based on our experience, and the existing research, we believe that social media is a fabulous option for building a sense of community in online learning. But we also want to caution that the needs of different cohorts of students differ, so the use of social media (just like any other teaching tool) may be more effective for some cohorts of online learners than it is for others.

5 Online Meetings

A fifth option for building community is through regularly scheduled synchronous meetings and learning activities (Lohmann et al., 2018; McInnerney & Roberts, 2004). Student learning outcomes in synchronous online learning are similar to the outcomes for face-to-face courses (Francescucci & Rohani, 2018). By providing a scheduled day and time when the instructor will be online to review coursework and/or provide a mini-lecture online, students have the chance to get to know one another, get to know their instructor, and get immediate responses to their questions. This is an easy way for students to feel as though they are part of a community and not isolated. Furthermore, by incorporating scheduled, online, live meetings with your students, you are incorporating regular and substantive interactions (RSI) into your classroom (see Introduction). By having students present their assignments or other activities and/or breaking your students into smaller groups, students also feel as though they are part of the course community (Berry, 2019; Knapp, 2018). Furthermore, Bolliger and Halupa (2012) found that many programs build community by hosting optional or required in-person meetings or socials. Research has also found that when students have opportunities to partake in asynchronous whole- and small-group discussions, they feel more connected (Berry, 2019; Rovai, 2007).

Approximately seven years ago, when Kathy was developing her online MEd programs, her university decided that instructors would offer weekly, one-hour virtual meetings for their online students as a way to build community within their courses and as a way to set the programs apart from other fully online programs. To this day, this is her favorite part of teaching online and one area that students say they are grateful for. Students report missing these virtual meetings when they are canceled or a student has to miss for other obligations; many students depend on these! Marla offers thirty-minute optional weekly meetings for each of her courses, and the students who attend report that they love the chance to get to know one another!

What faculty do in these meetings will differ depending on their needs, their students' needs, and even the expectations of the course. The meetings Kathy hosts are all a bit different depending on the subject. Some meetings are all about answering questions related to projects, others have a bit of lecture and assignment clarification, some include a review of what students will be covering, and some include breakout sessions where students can talk in small groups and then come back to the entire class to share what was discussed.

Marla starts her meeting with a sharing time that is unique to each cohort. A recent cohort of graduates had their children attend the first five minutes each week to share their news. In that five minutes, there was always conversation about lost teeth, spelling tests, and upcoming holidays. After the children left, the students spent the next twenty-five minutes listening to a short lecture and then getting questions answered. Other cohorts prefer to start with a lecture, followed by a Q&A time, and ending with sharing personal news.

Regardless of how you structure your online meetings, you are showing your students that you are available. Online meetings allow your students to interact with you, the course content, and their classmates—community building at its finest!

6 Opportunities for Student Collaboration

One way to build community in your online course is by having your students collaborate (Chatterjee & Correia, 2020). Han et al. (2022) also note the opposite impact—a sense of community can improve student collaboration. Based on the existing research, it is clear that giving students the opportunity to work together benefits their sense of community and feelings of connectedness to the course.

There are many ways you can provide opportunities for collaboration—your students can be as engaged as they, or you, want them to be. Encouraging students to create study groups is one effective way to build community among students in online courses. Students can create these study groups via GroupMeet, the discussion tools found in your LMS, or through many other tools that are available. In every course she teaches, Marla encourages students to form study groups, and she has witnessed the impact when they choose to do so. Frequently, she will receive emails with questions from a study group. Her courses involve students from all over the United States, and many of them meet in person for the first time at graduation. One of her favorite parts of graduation is watching these study groups hug one another and then head off for lunch together!

Online students can also collaborate by engaging in group projects. There are many ways this can look in online courses. It can be something students do asynchronously through the use of texting, emails, or even discussion boards, but what Kathy has found the most effective is encouraging, or requiring, that the groups meet a specified number of times via Zoom or some other synchronous means. Groups can be assigned, or you can allow students to sign up for their own groups. Kathy has used both and has not

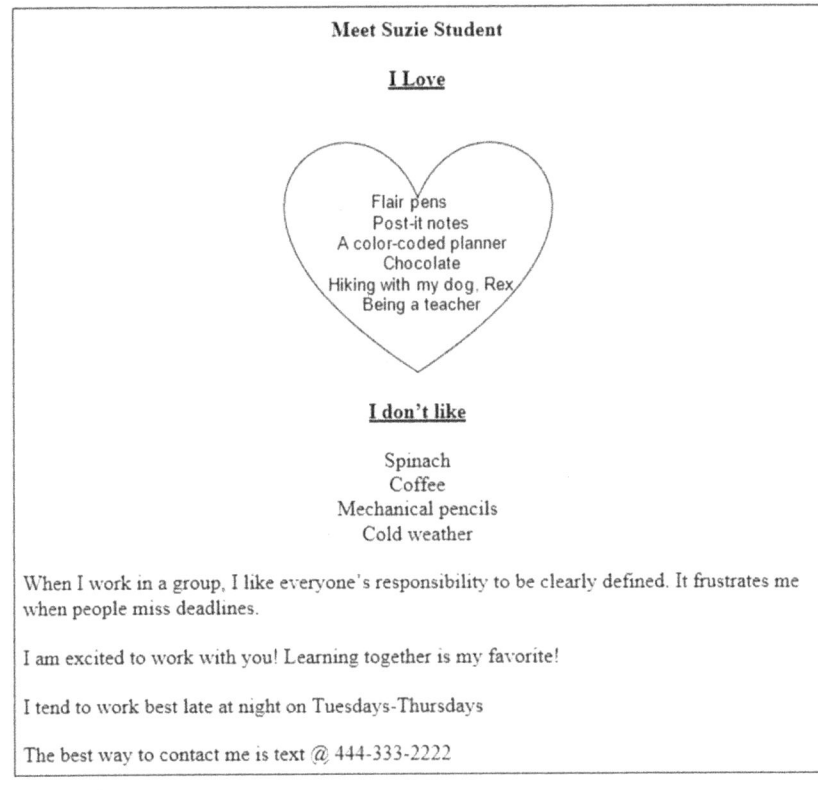

Figure 2.1 Sample Student Flyer for Group Project.

found one way that works any better than the other for her online students. If having students choose their own groups, one idea, learned from a different colleague, was to have students create simple flyers about themselves (see Figure 2.1). They can be very basic like the example or can include photographs and graphic designs.

Textbox 2.7

Book Study Project Sample Directions

You will be choosing a book to read and discuss in small groups. After your group has completed reading their book and completed the required discussions, you will be creating a presentation that you will give to another small group of students. The presentation piece is similar to a jigsaw discussion. In a jigsaw discussion, one person is the "expert" of the topic that they review. In your live presentations, you will be broken into groups that include one person from each book. You will then present or be the "expert" on your book and present your discussion group's presentation.

You will be doing the following:

1 Select a book, which automatically puts you into a group for your discussions.
2 Read the book and discuss with your small group via Zoom/Google Chat/InSpace.
3 Create a presentation.
4 Present your project.
5 Write a final reflection paper.
6 Complete a group member evaluation.
7 Turn in your group's presentation, your reflection paper, and your group member evaluation.

For more detailed directions and expectations, see the assignment directions in Blackboard.

The feedback Kathy has received when her students meet with their groups virtually, in real time, is always positive, and many students make lifelong friends afterward. The requirement for meetings may differ depending on the level of students you are teaching and/or the content being discussed. These group projects can entail anything—book studies, debate teams, jigsaw discussions, co-teaching lesson plans, professional learning communities, presentations, and the list goes on and on. You can also choose to require students to send in a recording of their meetings or not. When creating group projects, Kathy likes to use them sparingly. She also provides group member evaluation forms to the students. In her experience, Kathy's graduate students have been honest with their feedback regarding others' performance and in stating that when they hear the words "group project," a wall goes up and feelings of dread arise. By the end of the project, many students state that they actually find they enjoyed the project and learned a lot from their classmates and their experiences. Textbox 2.7 is an example of a group book study that can be easily adapted to fit the needs of your own particular course.

Community-Building Tools

Above are only a few samples of what the research and our experience have found to be helpful in building community. We chose these examples because we find they are some of the easiest ways to build community in the online classroom, as well as some of the most enjoyable. The tools mentioned in Table 2.1 are just a small sample of what can be used to assist you in the task of building community in your online classes. Throughout the last several years, we have tried all of these and change them up often (in fact, it is likely that we will have adapted how we use each of these tools between the writing of this book and its publication—teachers are lifelong learners who constantly grow in our knowledge!). We know there are many more tools out there, and we would love for you to share those tools with others and with us on social media using hashtag #OnlineTeacherPrep and tagging us! Just remember that the goal is to start small and add ideas each time you teach the course again—do not try to do it all at once.

Table 2.1 Tools for Building Community

	Name	Link
Polls	Poll Everywhere	https://www.polleverywhere.com
	Aweform	https://aweform.com
Informal discussions	Padlet	https://padlet.com
	Trello	https://trello.com
Social media	X (formerly Twitter)	https://x.com
	Facebook	https://www.facebook.com
Online meetings	InSpace	https://inspace.chat
	GoToMeeting	https://www.goto.com
Collaborative projects	Flock	https://www.flock.com
	Sync	https://www.sync.com

Avoid This

While it is important to be proactive and tell teachers what *to* do, we would be remiss if we didn't let you know what you should try to avoid. These are things we have personally done or seen/heard other instructors do that they have learned are not all that effective.

1 Forcing students to engage in optional community-building activities

As faculty members, we must remember that not all of our students want to, or are able to, be part of a community. Some students may just want to get in and out without any interaction—this is okay. Some of our students may be busy with countless commitments, such as multiple jobs, caregiving roles, extracurricular activities, and many other responsibilities. While it is great to show excitement and softly encourage students to engage in the activities, we must not force them to participate in optional community-building activities. In our experience, even the students who do not engage in the activities appreciate that we offer these options, and knowing that the community exists helps them feel more connected.

2 Assuming that all students need the same community aspects as their classmates

It is important to remember that we are teaching to a variety of students and a variety of student needs. Not all students will need or even want to engage in the same ways. This is important to remember when incorporating community-building activities into your online class. Remember to try and incorporate a variety of these strategies into your classes throughout the semester. This gives students options for how they want to engage, as well as when they choose to engage.

3 Over-monitoring student interactions with one another

As mentioned earlier, it is okay to not be involved in all aspects of your students' lives and schooling. We must learn to let go of the reins and trust our students. Allow them safe spaces to vent, problem-solve, and ask questions. Provide time to allow students to answer each other's questions. By taking a step back, we are teaching our students valuable skills such as how to read directions, collaborate, and problem-solve.

Let's Practice—"We Do"

Dr. Lopez is teaching an online Introduction to Education course. It is the first course in the degree program for many of his students, so Dr. Lopez does not know the students, and the students do not know one another. Dr. Lopez has taught this specific course a handful of times previously and has noticed that students frequently only interact with one another (and with him) when required to do so on the discussion board. And the previous course evaluations indicate that some students feel alone and disconnected from one another and from the university while taking the course. Dr. Lopez wants to change this and is looking for strategies that may aid him in building an online learning community among his students that will keep them engaged during this course and in future courses they may take together.

Textbox 2.8

1 Why should Dr. Lopez care that students feel isolated in his course?

2 Design an activity that Dr. Lopez can use during the first week of the course to begin building a learning community within the course.

3 Provide three specific practices that Dr. Lopez could use to support the learning community throughout the course.

4 Design an activity that Dr. Lopez can use to celebrate the learning community at the conclusion of the course.

Now it is time to practice. This is the "We Do" part of good teaching. Answer the questions in Textbox 2.8 using the blank spaces provided. Once you have your answers, share them on social media using the hashtag #OnlineTeacherPrep and tagging both of us in your post. You may also take a look at the suggestions in Appendix A if you get stumped (or need a little validation that you know what you are doing).

Apply to Your Own Courses—"You Do"

It is now time to practice building community in your own online course. Follow the steps in Textbox 2.9. Once you complete the steps, you will have one idea ready for immediate implementation in your next online course.

Textbox 2.9

1 Identify a course you teach. Write the name of the course here.

2 Choose one idea discussed in this chapter that you would like to implement in your online classroom. List the one strategy here.

3 Pull out your syllabus and look at the content—for which week or topic do you feel you can easily implement your strategy? Why do you want to start with this particular week or topic?

> **Textbox 2.9 (Continued)**
>
> 4 Create your activity and insert it into the appropriate place in your LMS. Write a brief summary of what you designed here.
>
> **Congratulations!**—You just started the process of building a sense of community in your online class! Now try it again for another course or another week in the same course.

References

Abdelmalak, M. M. M. (2015). Web 2.0 technologies and building online learning communities: Students' perspectives. *Online Learning, 19*(2), 1–20.

Benson, O. M., & Whitson, M. L. (2022). The protective role of sense of community and access to resources on college student stress and COVID-19-related daily life disruptions. *Journal of Community Psychology, 50*(6), 2746–2764. https://doi.org/10.1002/jcop.22817

Berry, S. (2018). Building community in an online graduate program: Exploring the role of an in-person orientation. *The Qualitative Report, 23*(7), 1673–1687. https://doi.org/10.46743/2160-3715/2018.3299

Berry, S. (2019). Faculty perspectives on online learning: The instructor's role in creating community. *Online Learning, 23*(4), 181–191. https://doi.org/10.24059/olj.v23i4.2038

Bolliger, D. U., & Halupa, C. (2012). Student perceptions of satisfaction and anxiety in an online doctoral program. *Distance Education, 33*(1), 81–98.

Boothe, K. A., Lohmann, M. J., Donnell, K., & Hall, D. D. (2018). Applying the principles of Universal Design for Learning in the college classroom. *Journal of Special Education Apprenticeship, 7*(3), Article 2.

Bosch, T. E. (2009). Using online social networking for teaching and learning: Facebook use at the University of Cape Town. *Communication, Cultural, and Media Studies, 35*(2), 185–200. https://doi.org/10.1080/02500160903250648

Chatterjee, R., & Correia, A. P. (2020). Online students' attitudes toward collaborative learning and sense of community. *American Journal of Distance Education, 34*(1), 53–68. https://www.tandfonline.com/doi/abs/10.1080/08923647.2020.1703479

Ervin-Kassab, L., & Drouin, S. (2021). Expert learning in (micro)communities of practice: A case study examining teacher professional development. *Professional Development in Education, 47*(4), 699–709. https://doi.org/10.1080/19415257.2021.1876145

Francescucci, A., & Rohani, L. (2018). Exclusively synchronous online (VIRI) learning: The impact on student performance and engagement outcomes. *Journal of Marketing Education, 41*, 60–69.

Han, J., Jiang, Y., Mentzer, N., & Kelley, T. (2022).The role of sense of community and motivation in the collaborative learning: An examination of the first-year design course. *International Journal of Technology and Design Education, 32*, 1837–1852. https://doi.org/10.1007/s10798-021-09658-6

Harris, H. S., & Martin, E. W. (2012). Student motivations for choosing online classes. *International Journal for the Scholarship of Teaching and Learning, 6*(2), Article 11. https://doi.org/10.20429/ijsotl.2012.060211

Huang, H. (2002). Toward constructivism for adult learners in online learning environments. *British Journal of Educational Technology, 33*(1), 27–37. https://doi.org/10.1111/1467-8535.00236

Jackson, S. H. (2019). Student questions: A path to engagement and social presence in the online classroom. *Journal of Educators Online, 16*(1).

Jacobs, J., & Archie, T. (2008). Investigating sense of community in first-year college students. *Journal of Experiential Education, 30*(3), 282–285. https://doi.org/10.1177/105382590703000312

Keis, O., Grab, C., Schneider, A., & Ochsner, W. (2017). Online or face-to-face instruction: A qualitative study on the electrocardiogram course at the University of Ulm to examine why students choose a particular format. *BMC Medical Education, 17*, Article 194. https://doi.org/10.1186/s12909-017-1053-6

Knapp, N. F. (2018). Increasing interaction in a flipped online classroom through video conferencing. *TechTrends, 62*, 618–624. https://doi.org/10.1007/s11528-018-0336-z

Knickle, K., & McNaughton, N. (2021). Who do I think you are? The guessing game ice breaker: Building community. *Medical Teacher, 43*(11), 1330–1332. https://doi.org/10.1080/0142159X.2021.1959025

Liu, N., Magjuka, R. J., Bonk, C. J., & Lee, S. (2007). Does sense of community matter? An examination of participants' perceptions of building learning communities in online courses. *Quarterly Review of Distance Education, 8*(1), 9–24, 87–88.

Lohmann, M. J., Boothe, K. A., Hathcote, A. R., & Turpin, A. (2018). Engaging graduate students in the online learning environment: A Universal Design for Learning (UDL) approach to teacher preparation. *Networks: An Online Journal for Teacher Research, 20*(2). https://doi.org/10.4148/2470-6353.1264

McInnerney, J. M., & Roberts, T. S. (2004). Collaborative or cooperative learning? In T. Roberts (Ed.), *Online collaborative learning: Theory and practice* (pp. 203–214). IGI Global. https://doi.org/10.4018/978-1-59140-174-2.ch009

Paxton, P. (2003). Inviting e-learning: How hard can it be? *Journal of Invitational Theory and Practice, 9*, 23–40.

Pike, G. R., Kuh, G. D., & McCormick, A. C. (2011). An investigation of the contingent relationships between learning community participation and student engagement. *Research in Higher Education, 52*, 300–322. https://doi.org/10.1007/s11162-010-9192-1

Rovai, A. P. (2007). Facilitating online discussions effectively. *The Internet and Higher Education, 10*(1), 77–88.

Splitter, L. J. (2009). Authenticity and constructivism in education. *Studies in Philosophical Education, 28*, 135–151. https://doi.org/10.1007/s11217-008-9105-3

Stone, C., O'Shea, S., May, J., Delahunty, J., & Partington, Z. (2016). Opportunity through online learning: Experiences of first-in-family students in online open-entry higher education. *Australian Journal of Adult Learning, 56*(2), 146–169.

3 Asynchronous Discussion Boards That Enhance Student Learning

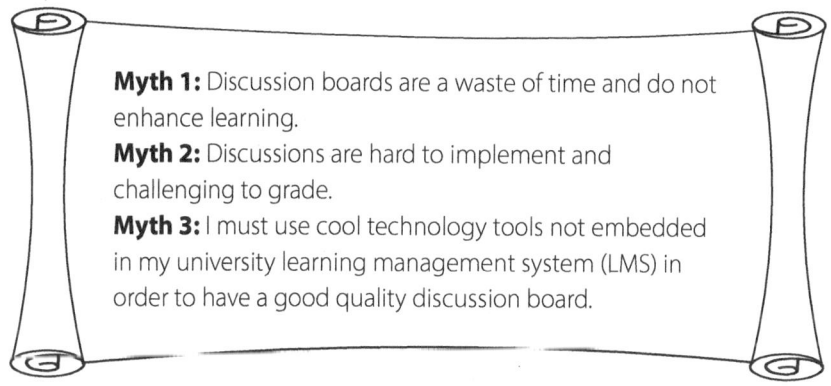

Myth 1: Discussion boards are a waste of time and do not enhance learning.
Myth 2: Discussions are hard to implement and challenging to grade.
Myth 3: I must use cool technology tools not embedded in my university learning management system (LMS) in order to have a good quality discussion board.

Debunking the Myths

We can only imagine what is going through your mind as you begin reading a chapter on discussion boards. Words like "yuck," "waste of time," "not gonna happen," or even "easy participation grade" are just a few that come to mind. We have heard from many colleagues, and from ourselves early in our online teaching journeys, that discussion boards are a waste of time and that students do not put effort into them. Some instructors and students alike think they are "gimme points" or "fluff work," and in many cases they are. However, this does not have to be the case. In the past few years, we both worked hard to create more engaging and helpful discussion boards. We have seen the benefits for our students, in terms of both engagement and the learning of concepts. In addition, we are having a lot more fun participating in, and grading, discussions these days. In fact, asynchronous online discussions are one of Marla's favorite parts of teaching!

The reality is that a well-designed online discussion board is a very effective teaching strategy, just as a good discussion can be in a face-to-face course. In the online classroom, the literature (e.g., Al Jeraisy et al., 2015; Romero et al., 2013) indicates that the use of discussion boards increases student learning in comparison to coursework that does not offer opportunities for interactive learning. Dahlstrom-Hakki et al. (2020) found that, for students with disabilities, comprehension of learning material was improved through the use of discussion boards, with asynchronous discussions leading to slightly higher learning comprehension than synchronous online discussions.

We also know that students see benefits to their learning when asynchronous discussion boards are used in online courses. Wu & Hiltz (2004) found that students perceive discussion boards to be effective learning tools and self-report that their own learning was enhanced through the use of this strategy, and Hamann et al. (2012) found that students prefer asynchronous online discussions to face-to-face discussions for sharing thoughts and having time to think before responding to classmates. This sentiment was reiterated by Meyer (2003), who states that students appreciate the additional time for reflection in online discussion boards in comparison to traditional face-to-face discussions. Finally, students report that the use of asynchronous discussion boards increases their sense of community within online courses (Lin & Gao, 2020). So, all that is to say that discussion boards are a valuable learning tool and are not a waste of time or busy work that distracts from learning. They are an effective learning tool in the online classroom!

A second myth we have heard is that discussions are hard to implement and challenging to grade. Like any effective teaching strategy, it can be hard work to do it well. In our experience, good teaching is (almost) never easy. But we should not shy away from hard work. And we believe that the hard work is worth the reward for online discussions!

Online discussions are most effective when faculty actively facilitate the discussion instead of simply observing the conversations emerging (Martin et al., 2020; Tanis, 2020; Xu et al., 2020). Effective facilitation strategies might include asking questions to further the conversation, affirming statements made by students, and encouraging deeper thoughts or critical thinking based on posts made by students (Tanis, 2020). That being said, Xu et al. (2020) also report that students within the course can emerge as discussion leaders and serve, at least in some capacity, to facilitate the asynchronous discussion, thus reducing the faculty workload.

In our experience, we do spend a considerable amount of time facilitating the discussion boards in our online courses. In fact, it is probably about one-fourth of the work we do in each course. So, implementing discussions is time-consuming work. But we do believe that, especially in asynchronous courses, we spend less time on other teaching tasks, such as offering live lectures and walking across campus to the classroom, so the facilitation of good discussions does not increase our workload over traditional face-to-face instruction.

As you will see below, we both like creative discussion boards in lieu of relying on traditional text-based discussions. And it turns out we are not alone in our preferences for varied discussion formats. Research indicates that college instructors are trying to vary the type of discussions they use in their online courses to keep students engaged and enhance learning (Ding et al., 2020; Lohmann & Boothe, 2020, 2024). But that creativity can be less straightforward to grade than more traditional discussion threads. However, with the use of high-quality rubrics and clear expectations for students, grading discussion boards is no more challenging than grading other learning assessments.

A third myth that has surfaced is that for discussions to be engaging and ensure student learning, faculty must use technology that is not part of the LMS. Each time Kathy and Marla attend a conference or talk to colleagues who are just starting to do online teaching, they hear conversations about technology tools that they use to support their asynchronous discussions. Tools such as FigJam, Padlet, and Flip are web-based applications that are popular among online instructors. Each of these tools is fantastic and offers wonderful ways for faculty to design discussions and for students to actively participate in those discussions. But the reality is that the use of these (or similar) tools is not necessary in order to have a high-quality discussion board. And in our experience, sometimes faculty focus more on finding the "right tool" than on creating a good discussion topic that will meet the learning objectives.

Depending on your LMS, there are several ways that you can make your discussions engaging without using outside technology. And many of the commonly used LMSs have tools built right into the discussion feature that eliminate the need to use outside tools. These are tools that students can use in drafting their initial discussion posts, as well as in responding to their classmates. D2L/Brightspace, Canvas, and Blackboard all have embedded tools that include (a) video integration, (b) uploading images and other files directly into the post so that they can be viewed within the post itself, (c) audio integration, and (d) traditional text, with the option to use varied fonts and text sizes.

The remainder of this chapter will review ways that we have made our discussion boards more effective and engaging for our students. Additionally, many of these ideas are things that your students can use in their current or future jobs. You will note that the tools we mention here are fewer in number, but the examples are abundant. This is because our passion lies in using various formats in our discussions.

Tools to Use—"I Do"

As you read the remainder of the chapter, identify ways you can make these ideas work for you and your courses' specific needs. Then feel free to share on social media and with your colleagues so that we can continue to build our online teaching toolboxes. Please remember to use the hashtag #OnlineTeacherPrep and tag both of us in your post.

1 Clear Guidelines of Expectations in Post

We all know that students do not always read instructions thoroughly. In truth, we often don't either. To ensure students understand our expectations, our instructions and guidelines for discussions must be clear and simple. Over the years, we have created many different discussion prompts and have found some things that are helpful when it comes to providing clear expectations. One thing we learned is that it is best to have the expectations clear in both the discussion board instructions *and* the rubric (ensuring that we provide the rubric to students along with the instructions). Textbox 3.1 provides an example of a discussion prompt Kathy uses in one of her courses.

Textbox 3.1

Discussion Prompt Example

After reading Chapter 2 in your textbook (*The Teacher's Guide to Action Research for Special Education in PK–12 Classrooms*), you should have a better understanding of action research and how to begin the process.

To start practicing, you will be using the case studies in Appendix B of your textbook. Before beginning, review the sample case studies found in Appendix A of your text.

For this week's discussion, **write a problem statement ONLY for the following case studies**. In your initial post and in your responses, clearly delineate the case study you are using.

Your responses should be modeled after the examples in the textbook, so it is vital that you take the time to carefully review those examples.

Case Study 1: Communication Delay in Preschool

Case Study 6: Transition Goal for High School Student

Your initial post is due **Thursday**, and your **3+ peer responses** are due **Sunday**. Please review the rubric for grading criteria.

When responding to peers, remember the following:

- Respond to 3 or more classmates with responses that further the discussion.
- Provide any useful feedback to assist them in improving their problem statements.
- Peer responses should include in-text citations as well as an APA-formatted reference section to support your suggestions. You must include at least 3 references, at least one of which must be peer reviewed.

When writing the expectations for your discussion posts, we recommend the following:

1. Use bullets when listing the expectations or bold the words that are most important for the students to see.
2. Keep the topic simple—don't ask students to respond to more than one or two discussions/prompts in each discussion.
3. Tell your students exactly what you want their response to look like.
4. Be clear about what you expect from the peer responses. This includes how many peers to respond to and the due date for the initial post and the peer responses. You may also want to include what specific information you are looking for in their peer responses, as well as whether references are needed.

In addition to providing clear instructions for each discussion, Marla has found it useful to provide overall discussion board guidance at the beginning of each course via a course announcement that she also sends as an email to all students. As she grades discussions throughout the course, she is able to point back to that guidance, in addition to the specific discussion board instructions and rubric. Textbox 3.2 is the course announcement/email that Marla shares with students in each course.

Textbox 3.2

Course Announcement of Discussion Expectations

Good morning, students, and happy Wednesday!

I want to help you succeed in this course and will post regular announcements with clarification on assignments and additional information that will enhance your learning. Today, I want to share the guidelines/expectations for the weekly discussions. Please note that these guidelines will apply in every course you will take in this program, so it is important that you familiarize yourself with the expectations.

- Each week, you need to submit your initial discussion post by Wednesday at 11:59 p.m. Mountain Time.

Textbox 3.2 (Continued)

- For each discussion, you need to respond to at least 5 classmates with thoughtful responses that continue the discussion by Sunday at 11:59 p.m. Mountain Time.
- You need to participate in the discussion on at least 3 separate days throughout the week. That means that you need to engage in the conversation on at least 1 day in addition to Wednesday and Sunday.
- Be sure that your responses to classmates further the discussion by asking questions directly related to their posts, sharing your experiences, offering resources on the topic, or continuing the discussion the classmate started.
- If your response to a classmate simply affirms what they said, you will receive 0 points for that response. While it is important to tell classmates when you agree with their statements, you must also tell them why you agree, supporting your statement with references. For example, you will get no points if your post says, "Nice work, Johnny! I agree!" A response that would earn points might look like this: "I agree with you, Johnny. In your post, you talked about how teachers should help students learn to ask for breaks and other calming tools when needed. According to Walker et al. (2021), students with emotional disabilities need to be explicitly taught self-advocacy skills. I think if this were my student, I would have him practice asking to go to the Calming Corner during times when he is not frustrated so that he knows how to ask when he needs it. How do you think you would teach the skill in your classroom?"
- There are no right or wrong answers to the discussion prompts. You are expected to develop your own answer to the question and support your answer with references and course materials. Your initial post should thoroughly answer the questions being asked and should provide unique insight on the issue. Please don't just repeat what you have read in the textbook or other course materials. Instead, give us a quick overview of the reading and then share what you think it means and how it might apply in your classroom or school.

(Continued)

> **Textbox 3.2 (Continued)**
>
> - It is very important to use APA-formatted citations in your discussions, including in-text citations and a reference section at the end of the post. With the exception of the "Getting to Know You" discussion, you are required to have references to support your statements in every discussion. Please note that this program uses the 7th edition of the APA manual.
> - The more you engage in the weekly discussion, the more you will learn in the course.
>
> Please let me know if you have any questions. Have a beautiful day!
>
> —Dr. Lohmann

2 Weekly Reflection Post

When she first started teaching online, Marla quickly discovered that students rush through online discussions, with their primary focus on meeting the required number of responses to classmates and other minimum requirements to get credit for participation. In her courses, initial posts are due on Wednesdays at 11:59 p.m., and responses to classmates are due on Sundays. She quickly noticed that most students posted their initial post sometime on Wednesday and their responses to classmates on Sunday evenings, but they did not engage in the discussion at other points in the week. Clearly, this is not the goal of discussions. The goal of discussion boards, just like the goal of any other learning activity, is to support student learning. So Marla began seeking ways to ensure that the discussions were more than "busy work" and led to student learning.

In the field of education, we frequently talk about the role of reflection in learning. Reflection on learning helps deepen students' understanding of the learning concepts (Helyer, 2015) and increases students' generalization and application of the content learned to other contexts (Kolb, 1984). Chang (2019) talks about integrating reflection into online courses; she found that the use of reflection helped students identify what they had learned and consider their own learning gaps.

To support student reflection on their own learning from the weekly discussion, encourage students to engage in the discussion beyond the minimum expectation, and ensure that students apply that learning to their own classrooms, Marla requires a reflection post at the end of each discussion—these are due on Sunday nights at the same time as the responses to classmates. Textbox 3.3 offers an example similar to what she uses in her discussion directions.

Textbox 3.3

Discussion Reflection Instructions

By Sunday evening at 11:59 p.m., post a reflection on your own learning from this discussion. Please adhere to the following guidelines for this requirement:

1 Title your post with the word "Reflection" followed by your name (example: "Reflection by Dr. Lohmann").

2 Share a 1–2 sentence summary of what you learned from this week's discussion, being sure that your summary does not simply parrot your initial post. Instead, it should demonstrate that you have read and considered both initial posts and responses from classmates.

3 Share your 3 big takeaways from this week's discussion. The takeaways you share might include any of the following:
   a New information you learned with an explanation of how that learning will impact your teaching practice
   b Statements made by classmates that changed your thinking on the topic, with a description of how that will impact your teaching practice
   c A question that you have on the discussion topic after participating in the discussion with your classmates

4 Be sure that your reflection post is focused on the discussion, not on other learning materials from the week.

5 Be sure to complete this requirement after fully participating in the discussion (including meeting the requirements for your initial post and responses to classmates).

In Marla's experience (and in her comparisons of courses with and without discussion reflections), using this strategy increases student engagement in the discussion overall and enhances student understanding of the topic being discussed. When students are asked to reflect on their learning and apply it to their classrooms, they must take the time to read and fully consider the posts of their classmates. In addition, they are actively looking for themes among statements made by classmates and thinking about how the topic being discussed directly applies to their classroom. We believe the discussion reflection strategy could also be used to assess student understanding and engagement after synchronous online discussions by asking students to submit a short document that answers the reflection questions posed.

3 Various Discussion Formats

We have saved the best (or at least what we consider the best part of designing online discussions) for last! The use of a variety of discussion board formats takes online course discussions to a whole new level. When we first started teaching online courses, we followed what we had seen others do and created all of our discussions using a traditional format in which students write a 300–400 word response to a question posed by the instructor and respond to their classmates with shorter written responses. We did not enjoy it, and neither did our students! Frankly, we often found ourselves avoiding participation in discussions (and not wanting to grade them) because it was boring and tedious work. Many of the students' initial posts were essentially the same, and it felt like we were simply reading twenty-five of the same thing!

In the last several years, we have begun to make changes to our discussion boards so that they are not all traditional text-based conversations. By doing so, we have increased student engagement and our own engagement in discussion boards and aligned our discussions with the Universal Design for Learning (UDL) principle of multiple means of action and expression. We still do some traditional text-based discussions, but we no longer rely on these as our primary means of student discussion.

We have tried a variety of discussion board formats and want to share a few of our favorites with you. Please do not think that this is an exhaustive list! In fact, the examples we are about to share are just the beginning, and we hope this information sparks your thinking to create your own discussion board formats (if it does, please share your ideas with us using hashtag #OnlineTeacherPrep and tag both of us in your post). Our favorite discussion board formats are having students (a) engage in a debate, (b) create a product they can use in their classroom or in interactions with families or colleagues, (c) create infographics or other visual representations, and (d) participate in video-based discussions. We offer examples of each of these formats below—you may notice that our examples do not include the discussion expectations. That is simply because we already demonstrated earlier in this chapter how we do that—for all of the varied discussion formats we recommend, we would use expectations similar to what we outlined earlier.

The first discussion format we will focus on is hosting a debate. Debates have been a common teaching strategy for centuries and were used in historical cultures including ancient Greece (Giorgini, 2019), ancient China (Kroll, 2015), and medieval Rome (Murphy, 2005). The use of debates in the classroom setting supports students in learning to analyze content and create logical arguments (Zare & Othman, 2013). In addition, debates support critical thinking and problem-solving skills (Park et al., 2011). Finally, in our experience, students really enjoy debates and are generally very engaged in these discussion boards, especially when the topic being debated is of high interest to the students.

There are several considerations when using debate-based discussion boards in the online classroom. First, this discussion strategy is best used when discussing a controversial topic in the field of education (Lohmann & Boothe, 2020, 2022). If there are not two very clear and opposing sides on the issue (with credible resources supporting both sides), students will find it very challenging to engage in a debate on the topic. Secondly, according to the Merriam-Webster (2024) online dictionary, a debate is "a regulated discussion of a proposition between two matched sides." This means that, when you design your debate, you must ensure that both sides have approximately the same number of students, as well as similar resources for debate preparation. Finally, you must consider whether you want each side of the debate to work as a team or whether each individual student should work on their own. When students work as a team, they are better able to make a strong case for their side. But coordinating time to collaborate and build a case can be challenging, especially in fully asynchronous courses. As you consider the use of debate-based discussions in your own classrooms, we want to share an example in Textbox 3.4.

Textbox 3.4

Debate Discussion on Cell Phone Use

Over the past few weeks, we have been talking about technology use in the middle school classroom. As you have learned, there are a variety of viewpoints regarding technology and its role in instruction. In the middle school classroom, student access to personal technology devices is often considered controversial. For this week's discussion, we will be engaging in a debate on the topic of cell phone use in the middle school classroom. Here is what you need to know in order to participate in this discussion:

1 Group 1 needs to argue that students should have unlimited access to cell phones at any point in the school day.

2 Group 2 needs to argue that students should have no access to cell phones during school hours.

3 You may not agree with the stance of your assigned group, but you need to argue for the side you were assigned.

4 Your initial post should be your "opening arguments" in the debate. Make your case for your assigned stance and be sure to cite at least 3 credible sources on the topic.

5 Respond to at least 3 peers who have been assigned the opposing stance. In those replies, offer a strong rebuttal to your classmates' statements, being sure to cite at least 1 credible source in each rebuttal.

6 Respond to at least 3 peers who have been assigned to the same stance as you. In those replies, offer additional information to support what your classmate said.

7 Group 1 is the following students: Adams, Brown, Dunkin, Flores, Hall, Johnson, Martinez, Parker, Richardson, Singh, Taylor, and Yang.

8 Group 2 is the following students: Armstrong, Davis, Eastman, Garcia, Hansen, King, Nguyen, Poole, Ruiz, Smith, Thomas, and Zhu.

A second type of discussion we like to include in our courses is having students create products that they can use in their classroom (Lohmann & Boothe, 2020, 2022). Including this discussion format can increase student mastery of the course content (Mathew & Alid-mat, 2013). For example, in Kathy's undergraduate course, she has her students create a newsletter that discusses what positive behavior interventions and supports (PBIS) are; information on why they are using PBIS in their class; and information for parents about the classroom rules, procedures, consequences, and reward system that will be used (an example of this is given in Appendix B). The students are told to also include information about how parents can help support their classroom management system at home. This can then be shared in the discussion thread. Similarly, in her Classroom Management course, Marla has students create a classroom expectations poster that outlines 3–5 behavior expectations for their classrooms. Students create a JPEG of the poster for the discussion board and then are encouraged to use a full-size version of the poster in their own classrooms. Other examples of products that students might create and share in a class discussion include (a) lesson plans, (b) worksheets or other assignments, (c) letters to parents/caregivers, (d) behavior plans, (e) individualized education programs (IEPs), and (f) résumés or cover letters for job applications.

Because this discussion format is less about discussing and more focused on sharing ideas and offering feedback to one another, students may need explicit guidance on how to respond to their peers. We always encourage students to offer specific (but kind and respectful) feedback to their classmates on the product, identifying both the positives of the products and areas for improvement. Because not all students know how to do this or what to consider in these discussions, Marla offers a list of questions to consider when responding to classmates as given in Textbox 3.5.

A third discussion format is having students create infographics to communicate the key information related to a learning topic. Infographics are visual representations of information and should be visually appealing and make it easier for stakeholders to understand the information (Canva, 2024). Infographics are an effective tool to increase active learning and engagement with the course content (Jaleniauskiene & Kasperiuniene, 2023) and for students to share information with one another (Tarkhova et al., 2020). In addition, students report that the use of infographics increases their own learning and is an enjoyable method of presenting content (Grieger & Leontyev, 2021).

> **Textbox 3.5**
>
> ### Questions to Consider
>
> 1. What is the objective of the product? What function does it serve in the teacher's classroom?
> 2. What have we learned in this course or previous courses about similar products?
> 3. In what ways does the product align with what we have learned is best practice?
> 4. In what ways does the product not align with best practice?
> 5. What additional positives do you see with the product?
> 6. How can you point out these positives using specific praise and describing why you believe they are positives?
> 7. What additional areas for improvement do you see with the product?
> 8. How can you identify these areas for improvement in a manner that is specific and respectful?

In our experience, infographics help our students learn to synthesize their learning and to be succinct in communicating their message to others. When we use these types of assignments, we have noticed that students initially have one of two reactions—either they are excited because they enjoy making infographics or want to learn to create them, or they are incredibly nervous because they fear not having the technology skills to do a good job. Marla has found that participating in infographic discussions with her students by creating her own simple infographic and posting an initial post early in the week helps to calm the fears of students who are anxious about this task. When they see that she does not necessarily make fancy visual representations (but still infographics that meet the requirements and effectively share information in a visually appealing way), students often realize that they can do it too. Similarly, Kathy has a Google folder that has example infographics and blogs, articles, and videos on ways to create infographics and a list of certain software they can use to create them.

In our courses, we use infographic discussions in a few ways: (a) students create infographics that they could later use in their classrooms to communicate information to caregivers or colleagues; (b) students essentially do a jigsaw discussion, with each student reading a different article or researching a different topic and then creating an infographic to share what they learned with their classmates; and (c) students share about their capstone research projects through an infographic. When students create infographics, they upload them as JPG or PNG files into the discussion board and ensure that their classmates can view the file without needing to download it. Textbox 3.6 offers an example discussion for creating infographics that students might use to communicate information to the caregivers of their students.

At this point, we also want to share one other strategy we really like to use in our discussion boards—the element of choice (discussed fully in Chapter 1). Not every student needs to respond to the discussion prompt in the same manner. As long as all students are able to achieve the learning objective, the participation format should not matter! Whenever possible, we try to use the UDL framework to inform our course design and instruction; we know that the use of choice is strongly supported in the UDL framework and that UDL Consideration 7.1 is to "optimize choice and autonomy" (CAST, 2024).

Textbox 3.6

Infographic Discussion

This week, we learned about the special education procedural safeguards, and you heard that it is the responsibility of the school to ensure that families receive this document at least once per year. You also learned that it can be challenging for many families to understand this document. For this discussion, pretend that you are a special education advocate and you seek to support families in understanding their rights. Create a one-page infographic that outlines the procedural safeguards.

Kathy has taken the infographic discussion format and expanded on it by utilizing choice where students can choose to create an infographic or a TikTok-like video to demonstrate their understanding of the content. Marla often creates discussions in which she poses a topic and tells students they can post their initial post and responses in a manner of their own choosing and offers examples of ways students might choose to post, including (a) text, (b) video, (c) infographic, (d) comic strip, (e) poem, (f) drawing, (g) musical rendition, and (h) mock social media post. Students report enjoying the ability to highlight their own talents and seeing the various skills of classmates in choice-based discussions. And, as faculty members, we really enjoy these choice discussions—they are fun to facilitate and interesting to grade!

The final discussion format we want to discuss is the use of video-based discussions. This discussion format has been shown to increase engagement in student learning (Lohmann & Boothe, 2022; Swartzwelder et al., 2019) and increase student connectedness and social presence in the online classroom (Milovic & Dingus, 2021; Murphy et al., 2021). Our students report that they enjoy seeing each other's faces and hearing each other's voices in these discussions. And, as faculty teaching asynchronous online courses, these discussions are sometimes the only opportunity we have to "put a face to a name" with our students.

When designing video-based discussion, you will need to clearly communicate the expectations for the video. Make sure students know whether they are expected to give a presentation (e.g., use a PowerPoint or Google Slides presentation) or simply speak. Set a clear length expectation for the videos—without this, some students will post one-minute videos and others will post twenty-minute videos. And offer resources to help students learn to record videos, especially if this tool is embedded in your LMS and they are able (or even expected) to record their video directly in the discussion tool. On a related note, if your LMS offers the video tool embedded in the discussions, we highly recommend having students do their videos using that tool, as this means their classmates do not have to click an external link or download a file to view the video.

Finally, we suggest being open when students communicate privacy concerns about participating in a video-based discussion—when this happens, we suggest offering an alternative assignment for that student, if possible. Marla has offered to let students simply do a voice-over PowerPoint video or use an avatar to speak in the video. Additionally, you want to ensure that the video can be reviewed by all, so we suggest to our students that they include either a transcript or to close-caption their video.

We have used video-based discussions for a variety of topics in our courses. Some examples include:

- Creating a video model of a classroom task that our students could later use in their own classrooms.
- Teaching a mock five-minute asynchronous mathematics lesson—with the increase in "remote learning days" in lieu of "snow days," we are finding that our students need to know how to teach their PK–12 students in a virtual classroom.
- Conducting a mock webinar for classroom paraprofessionals on classroom interventions.
- A three-minute thesis to describe students' master's capstone research project.
- A task analysis where students write out the steps of their task analysis for teaching a specific skill and then record themselves teaching the skill following their task analysis steps.
- Creating a TikTok-style video to share the truth that learning styles are an educational myth (see Textbox 3.7).
- A Teacher Sizzle, similar to CIDDL's Cizzle (https://ciddl.org/ciddl-cizzles-gamified-professional-development/), that has students identify a recipe that they can relate an instructional strategy to and discuss the similarity between the steps of the recipe and the strategy as they make their recipe.

As you begin planning for innovative and creative discussion boards, we want to share our tips for using each of the discussion board formats we have discussed. Please see Table 3.1 for our recommended considerations for each discussion board format. While we briefly discussed each of the four discussion board formats, we barely started sharing what we believe you should know on this topic! For even more information on asynchronous online discussion boards, check out our book chapters and articles on this very topic—you can find some of our articles in the resources found at the end of the chapter or you can simply do a Google Scholar search for either of us to find more (just a word of warning, though: We LOVE discussion boards and have published several articles on this topic, so you will find a lot of

Textbox 3.7

Sample Video-Based Discussion

This week you have read a bit on learning styles and also learned that learning styles are a myth. In this week's discussion, you must help debunk the learning styles myth. MAKE IT BELIEVABLE!

Create a TikTok to share with colleagues that helps debunk the learning styles myth. For more information on creating TikToks, click HERE. Your TikTok-like video should be no more than 3 minutes. If you are not creating a true TikTok, I suggest using Yuja, which is embedded in Canvas, to complete this activity.

Once you have created your TikTok, please post it to this discussion thread and respond to at least 3 peers. You will not be able to see your peers' posts until you have posted your initial discussion. Both your initial post and peer responses are due on **Sunday**. In your peer responses, make sure to support your responses with research. This means you need citations/references.

Table 3.1 Considerations and Tips for Using Various Discussion Board Formats

Discussion Board Format	Tips for Use
Debate	• Use when there is an opportunity where students need to defend their position. • Ensure they include research support.
Product creation	• Use when there is a product that your students can use in their own classroom. • Ensure students know why this product is important to them in their classroom and how it can enhance student learning/collaboration.
Infographics	• Use when there are several strategies, etc. that need to be covered. • Use when you are covering a large amount of material.
Video-based discussion	• Use when students need to model a particular skill (e.g., task analysis). • Use for students to present a topic to their classmates.

Table 3.2 Discussion Format Tools

Name	Link
Canva (infographics)	https://www.canva.com/create/infographics
Adobe Express (infographics)	https://www.adobe.com/express/templates/infographic
ScreenPal (video based)	https://screenpal.com
Yuja (video based)	https://www.yuja.com
Book Creator (product creation)	https://bookcreator.com
Adobe Express Lesson Plan Maker (product creation)	https://www.adobe.com/express/create/planner/lesson

self-citations in the additional resources in Appendix H—don't judge us too harshly for our shameless self-citation!).

Discussion Tools

Above, we provided ways to change your discussions to make them more engaging, but most of our time was spent on different discussion formats that can be used to vary the way your students demonstrate their understanding of the content that may be more practical than "Give a prompt, answer a prompt, and respond to 2+ peers." Table 3.2 provides several tools we provide to our students as they complete different discussion activities. There are definitely more programs that can assist your students with their discussions, and we would love for you to share. Please share the tools that you and your students have found helpful (#OnlineTeacherPrep and tag both of us in your post).

Avoid This

While it is important to be proactive and tell teachers what *to* do, we would be remiss if we didn't let you know what you should try to avoid when creating online discussion boards. Below, we share the top faculty behaviors we recommend avoiding in online discussion boards.

1 Relying only on text-based discussions

After teaching online for the past several years, we have found that providing students opportunities to demonstrate their learning in different ways allows them to shine! Not all students, even graduate students, are good writers. When we design all discussions to be text based, we are essentially asking our students to write, and share, a paper every single week. If our instructional goal is a paper, we could simply assign a paper instead of a discussion. Plus, relying on only text-based discussions can be VERY boring for you and for your students!

2 Treating online discussion boards like course assignments

We want to ensure that you understand that discussion boards are not meant to be long-winded assignments in which students demonstrate mastery of the course content. While we do suggest that you take a grade on the discussion, it does not have to be as many points as other assignments, and a large percentage of the grade should be based on student interaction, not just the initial discussion post. We also suggest that you require citations and references, especially for graduate students, so they can begin learning how to cite correctly and back up what they are saying. But, when doing this, don't expect students to format everything using APA guidelines. Marla generally has students put an APA-formatted reference section at the end of discussion posts (especially the initial post), but the primary focus is on the fact that students can support their statements with references. It is also important to recognize that if students are writing their responses directly into the discussion thread, the LMS may not allow for proper formatting.

3 Not being a part of the discussion

We mentioned in the Introduction the importance of regular and substantive interactions (RSIs) and the importance of being actively engaged in your online courses (see Chapter 1). By responding to student discussion posts, you can help clarify content, but you can also model to your students the expectations for peer response posts. We have found that students do not engage in their discussions as much when we are not engaged. They think it will be an easy A assignment if we are not in the discussion regularly and responding to posts. We are not saying you must respond to every student's posts, but it is important that throughout the week you respond to several and try to clear up any misconceptions or false information that may be shared by students in the discussion. You want your students to see you in the class engaged in what they are doing and learning.

Let's Practice—"We Do"

Dr. Bullock's online teaching methods class is currently learning about using technology tools to support instruction. He wants students to demonstrate their learning by applying their knowledge. Each student is currently doing their second field experience course and working on writing lessons for future observations. Dr. Bullock would like to create a discussion board that will help students apply what they are learning about instructional technology to their own field placements. His objective for the discussion is that all students will be able to appropriately integrate one technology support into their next lesson observation in a manner that supports the learning of the children in the classroom.

Now it is time to practice. This is the "We Do" part of good teaching. Use the vignette above to answer the questions in Textbox 3.8 using the blank spaces provided. Once you have your answers, share them on social media using the hashtag #OnlineTeacherPrep and tagging both of us in your post. You may also take a look at the suggestions in Appendix A if you get stumped (or need a little validation that you know what you are doing).

Apply to Your Own Courses—"You Do"

It is now your time to practice creating unique and engaging discussions for your own online course. Follow the steps in Textbox 3.9. Once you complete the steps, you will have one idea ready to implement in your next online course.

Textbox 3.8

1. Select a discussion format that would be appropriate for this planned discussion and would support the students in achieving the learning objective outlined by Dr. Bullock.

2. What barriers might students face in completing this discussion? How should Dr. Bullock proactively prevent those barriers?

3. What supports or additional information might Dr. Bullock need to give his students to be able to complete your chosen discussion format?

Textbox 3.9

1. Identify a course you teach in which you want to add or change discussion boards.

2. Once the course is identified and you have a chosen discussion format, pull out your syllabus and look at the content—for which week(s) or topic(s) do you feel you can easily adapt your original discussion board prompt?

3. Make a list of your week(s) and/or topic(s), and next to each one write which discussion format you want to use. We suggest starting with something easy—a course you know is easy and a discussion format that is not too far outside your own comfort zone.

4. Now choose one of your week(s)/topic(s) and create your new discussion prompt. Determine if having your students self-reflect on this prompt is important or not—if so, add it; if not, simply move on to the next week(s)/topic(s).

(Continued)

> **Textbox 3.9 (Continued)**
>
> 5 Lastly, think back to what we wrote about writing clear expectations for both the initial post and students' responses to classmates. Make changes to your expectations to make them clearer for your students.
>
> 6 If needed, adapt your rubric to match the discussion prompt—remember to focus on the content more than the method. OR you may choose to do work on this after reading Chapter 6 where we discuss rubrics!
>
> **Congratulations!**—You just created an engaging discussion prompt for your online class! Now try it again for another course or another topic or week.

References

Al Jeraisy, M. N., Mohammad, H., Fayyoumi, A., & Alrashideh, W. (2015). Web 2.0 in education: The impact of discussion board on student performance and satisfaction. *Turkish Online Journal of Educational Technology, 14*(2), 247–258.

Canva. (2024). *How to make an infographic—ultimate guide.* https://www.canva.com/learn/how-to-make-an-infographic/

CAST (2024). *Universal Design for Learning guidelines* (Version 3.0). https://udlguidelines.cast.org

Chang, B. (2019). Reflection in learning. *Online Learning, 23*(1), 95–110. https://doi.org/10.24059/olj.v23i1.1447

Dahlstrom-Hakki, I., Alstad, Z., & Banerjee, M. (2020). Comparing synchronous and asynchronous online discussions for students with disabilities: The impact of social presence. *Computers and Education, 150*. https://doi.org/10.1016/j.compedu.2020.103842

Ding, L., Kim, C. M., & Orey, M. (2020). Design of gamified asynchronous online discussions. *Technology, Pedagogy, and Education, 29*(5), 631–647. https://doi.org/10.1080/1475939X.2020.1801495

Giorgini, G. (2019). Does democracy necessarily rest on relativism? The origins of the debate in Ancient Greece. In C. Riedweg (Ed.), *Philosophie für die Polis. Akten des 5. Kongresses der Gesellschaft für antike Philosophie 2016* (pp. 93–120). De Gruyter. https://doi.org/10.1515/9783110664836-005

Grieger, K., & Leontyev, A. (2021). Student-generated infographics for learning green chemistry and developing professional skills. *Journal of Chemical Education, 98*(9), 2881–2891. https://doi.org/10.1021/acs.jchemed.1c00446

Hamann, K., Pollock, P. H., & Wilson, B. M. (2012). Assessing student perceptions of the benefits of discussions in small-group, large-class, and online learning contexts. *College Teaching, 60*(2), 65–75. https://doi.org/10.1080/87567555.2011.633407

Heyler, R. (2015). Learning through reflection: The critical role of reflection in work-based learning (WBL). *Journal of Work Applied Management, 7*(1), 15–27. https://doi.org/10.1108/JWAM-10-2015-003

Jaleniauskiene, E., & Kasperiuniene, J. (2023). Infographics in higher education: A scoping review. *E-Learning and Digital Media, 20*(2), 191–206. https://doi.org/10.1177/20427530221107774

Kolb, D. A. (1984). *Experiential learning: Experience as the source of learning and development*. Prentice-Hall.

Kroll, J. L. (2015). Disputation in ancient Chinese culture. *Early China, 11*, 118–145. https://doi.org/10.1017/S0362502800003989

Lin, X., & Gao, L. (2020). Students' sense of community and perspectives of taking synchronous and asynchronous online courses. *Asian Journal of Distance Education, 15*(1), 169–179. https://www.asianjde.com/ojs/index.php/AsianJDE/article/view/448

Lohmann, M. J., & Boothe, K. A. (2020). Developing asynchronous online discussion boards to increase student engagement and learning. In R. Ceglie, A. Thornburg, & D. Abernathy (Eds.), *Handbook of research on developing engaging online courses* (pp. 134–151). IGI Global.

Lohmann, M. J., & Boothe, K. A. (2022). Using asynchronous discussions to teach classroom management skills in online teacher preparation courses. *Journal of Special Education Preparation, 2*(3), 48–58.

Lohmann, M. J., & Boothe, K. A. (2024). Supporting student engagement through the use of three discussion formats in a graduate teacher education course. *Journal of the American Academy of Special Education Professionals, 25*(1). https://doi.org/10.4148/2470-6353.1376

Martin, F., Wang, C., & Sadaf, A. (2020). Facilitation matters: Instructor perception of helpfulness of facilitation strategies in online courses. *Online Learning, 24*(1), 28–49. https://doi.org/10.24059/olj.v24i1.1980

Mathew, N. G., & Alidmat, A. O. H. (2013). A study on the usefulness of audio-visual aids in EFL classroom: Implications for effective instruction. *International Journal of Higher Education, 2*(2), 86–91. https://doi.org/10.5430/ijhe.v2n2p86

Merriam-Webster Dictionary. (2024). *Debate.* https://www.merriam-webster.com/dictionary/debate

Meyer, K. A. (2003). Face-to-face versus threaded discussions: The role of time and higher-order thinking. *Journal of Asynchronous Learning Networks, 7*(3), 55–65.

Milovic, A., & Dingus, R. (2021). How to not disappear completely: Using video-based discussions to enhance student social presence in an online course. *Marketing Education Review, 31*(4), 311–321. https://doi.org/10.1080/10528008.2021.1943447

Murphy, J., Swartzwelder, K., Serembus, J., Roch, S., Maheu, S., Rockstraw, R., & Leggieri, A. (2021). Text-based versus video discussions to promote a sense of community: An international mixed methods study. *Journal of Educators Online, 18*(3), Article 3.

Murphy, J. J. (2005). *Latin rhetoric and education in the Middle Ages and Renaissance.* Routledge.

Park, C., Kier, C., & Judgev, K. (2011). Teaching strategy in online education: A case study. *Canadian Journal of Learning and Technology, 37*(3), 1–17.

Romero, C., Lopez, M. I., Luna, J. M., & Ventura, S. (2013). Predicting students' final performance from participation in online discussion forums. *Computers & Education, 68*, 458–472. https://doi.org/10.1016/j.compedu.2013.06.009

Swartzwelder, K., Murphy, J., & Murphy, G. (2019). The impact of text-based and video discussions on student engagement and interactivity in an online course. *Journal of Educators Online, 16*(1), 1–7.

Tanis, C. J. (2020). The seven principles of online learning: Feedback from faculty and alumni on its importance for teaching and learning. *Research in Learning Technology, 28*, 2319. https://journal.alt.ac.uk/index.php/rlt/article/view/2319/2664

Tarkhova, L., Tarkhov, S., Nafikov, M., Akhmetyanov, I., Gusev, D., & Akhmarov, R. (2020). Infographics and their application in the educational process. *International Journal of Emerging Technologies in Learning (iJET), 15*(13), 63–80. https://www.learntechlib.org/p/217600/

Walker, J. D., Johnson, K. M., & Randolph, K. M. (2021). Teacher self-advocacy for the shared responsibility of classroom and behavior management. *TEACHING Exceptional Children, 53*(3), 216–225. https://doi.org/10.1177/0040059920980481

Wu, D., & Hiltz, S. R. (2004). Predicting learning from asynchronous online discussions. *Journal of Asynchronous Learning Networks, 8*(2), 139–152.

Xu, B., Chen, N. S., & Chen, G. (2020). Effects of teacher role on student engagement in WeChat-based online discussion learning. *Computers & Education, 157*. https://doi.org/10.1016/j.compedu.2020.103956

Zare, P., & Othman, M. (2013). Classroom debate as a systematic teaching/learning approach. *World Applied Sciences Journal, 28*(11), 1506–1513.

4 Implementing Remote Observations of Field Experiences into Online Programming

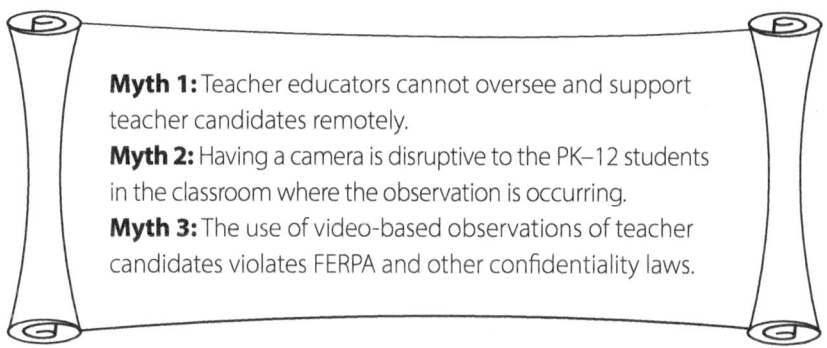

Myth 1: Teacher educators cannot oversee and support teacher candidates remotely.
Myth 2: Having a camera is disruptive to the PK–12 students in the classroom where the observation is occurring.
Myth 3: The use of video-based observations of teacher candidates violates FERPA and other confidentiality laws.

Debunking the Myths

When Marla tells people that her university uses remote observations for field experiences, she receives one of two responses. Either people are fascinated and want to know more. Or they immediately question how a remote field experience could be effective and how teacher educators can possibly oversee teacher candidates when they don't observe them in person. This myth that sufficient observation can only occur in person is pervasive. But it is just that—a myth.

The reality is that teacher coaching and observation lead to improved teacher pedagogical behaviors (Cohen et al., 2020; Crawford et al., 2021; Kraft et al., 2018). And, like other aspects of remote instruction, observations can be effectively implemented remotely. Over the past few decades, universities have been using technology tools to offer structured teaching simulations for teacher candidates and in-service teachers, using tools such as Mursion (Dalinger et al., 2020; Horn et al., 2023) and TeachLivE (Dieker et al., 2015; Ersozlu et al., 2021). Through the use of these tools, both teacher candidates and university teacher education faculty have grown their capacity and skills for using technology to support supervision and coaching in the classroom. In our experience, teacher educators no longer question the validity of using these mixed-reality simulation tools for coaching and supervision purposes. We posit that the use of remote observations of field experiences is similar to mixed reality and can lead to similar impacts on teacher candidate skill development.

Ault et al. (2019) compared remote observations and face-to-face observations for the same pool of teacher candidates. They found that students received similar feedback on observations in both formats. Similarly, Wake et al. (2017) report that teacher candidates doing their field experiences in rural settings benefited from the frequent and immediate feedback that occurred through the use of virtual observations. With this information in mind, we believe that remote observations of field experiences can be just as effective as more traditional teacher candidate observations, but they will look different from what many teacher educators are accustomed to.

At this time, we also want to point out that the remote observations that many universities conducted in the spring of 2020, due to the COVID-19 lockdowns, were not the norm for high-quality remote field experiences. We believe that some of the concern and pushback, and the perpetuation of the myth that remote observations are ineffective, are based on misconceptions from experiences that university faculty, teacher candidates, and host schools had during that time period. So this is our gentle reminder to all readers that spring 2020 was "emergency remote teaching," and what we all experienced that spring, and the following summer and fall, is not representative of what online learning can or should be.

The second myth we have heard regarding remote observation is that the PK–12 students will be distracted by the camera and other technology equipment in the classroom, thus making the observation inauthentic. According to the literature (Liang, 2015; Mac Mahon et al., 2019; Onyett, 2011), the opposite is actually true, and the presence of an observer in the classroom itself is more disruptive to students than a video camera. The reality is that over 90% of PK–12 classrooms in the United States rely on technology tools for classroom instruction on a regular basis (Gray & Lewis, 2021), and the use of technology for instruction is considered a vital practice for effective instruction in today's schools (Hoch et al., 2024). Children are accustomed to seeing, and using, a variety of technology tools in their schools and classrooms. It is likely that many of their classrooms already include video cameras or other tools, such as tablets or smartphones, that can be used for video-recording purposes.

In our experience, students will initially express interest in the camera and the fact that they are being video recorded. When teachers take the time to discuss with them why the video camera is there, they quickly get accustomed to its presence, and the classroom activities continue as normal. Because some students can be initially distracted by the camera, though, we do recommend that teacher educators consider this when viewing the first one or two video observations submitted by a teacher candidate in any given classroom setting. We suggest treating the student's initial interest in the camera much like we do when children approach us during face-to-face observations to ask, "Who are you?" or "Why are you here?"—or to share a story about their missing tooth or their pet cat who ate their pet fish!

Finally, teacher educators have expressed concerns that the use of video-based remote observations can violate FERPA and other confidentiality laws. While we understand this concern (and had very similar concerns ourselves when we first started teaching online), we have come to realize that with good protocols and protections in place, there is no need for concern. The Family Educational Rights and Privacy Act, commonly known as FERPA, is a federal law that ensures families have rights to access their children's school records and the right to ensure that personal information about their child and their family is kept confidential (United States Department of Education, 2021). Under the guidance from the United States Department of Education (n.d.), this law applies to video recordings in which the video is "directly related" to the student; their guidance suggests, but does not explicitly state, that if the teacher candidate is the focus of the video, there are no FERPA violations. With that being said, we highly suggest that teacher educators consult with their university legal counsel on this topic.

If there are any concerns about potential FERPA violations, we have seen a few strategies that universities have successfully used. First, some teacher education programs work with the host school to gain permission from all caregivers of the PK–12 students for the use of video observations. Second, some host schools use the photo/video release forms they routinely send to families in registration information to indicate that students in a given classroom may be video recorded. And, thirdly, when permission cannot be granted for video recording of students, the webcam can be aimed at just the teacher so that only he/she is included in the video. We suggest finding the strategy that works best for both the teacher education program and the host school and ensuring that the video software you select has confidentiality protocols in place so that the videos can only be viewed by approved individuals. For example, for live remote observations, you should ensure that the users must have a password to get into the meeting space so that strangers cannot simply find a link and join. In addition, we would not recommend having students upload their video recordings for asynchronous observations to tools such as YouTube that can be accessed easily by others.

Tools to Use—"I Do"

There are a number of ways that teacher educators can implement remote observation. Here, we share three of our favorite strategies for ensuring a positive learning experience through remote field experience observation.

1 Self-Reflection

We know that self-reflection is vital for teacher candidates (Black, 2015; Slade et al., 2019). Teacher candidates who engage in self-reflection, either individually or with colleagues, are more effective in the classroom and show an increase in student achievement (Kheirzadeh & Sistani, 2018; Miller, 2023). In addition, the use of reflective practices for in-service teachers can support teachers in identifying their own areas for professional growth and increasing their skills in the classroom (Moayeri & Rahimiy, 2019), and it can assist university faculty in identifying areas of need for individualized coaching for each student (Altalhab et al., 2020).

Van Boxtel (2017) found that teacher candidates and their cooperating teachers report that asynchronous video-based observations increase opportunities for self-reflection on teaching strengths and areas for growth.

These findings were reiterated by Chilton and McCracken (2017). The increase in self-reflection is likely due to the fact that teacher candidates are able to watch themselves teach and can watch the video multiple times or at various speeds to gain a better understanding of themselves as teachers.

When we prepare teacher candidates for self-reflection, we must be prepared for the fact that most of us are our own worst critics—watching themselves teach can be very challenging and somewhat discouraging. It is likely that many of your students will see their own teaching videos and see nothing but problems. In fact, we would venture to guess that a few of them will come to the conclusion that they are horrible teachers and need to find a new major. Be prepared for this and proactively prevent it as much as possible. There is no perfect teacher, and you are certainly not expecting perfection from any of your teacher candidates—be sure to communicate this fact to them! If you are willing to do so, it can help some students to hear about your own teaching weaknesses and areas for improvement. Another way to support teacher candidates in reducing their unrealistic expectations of their own teaching is to have them practice by first reflecting on videos of others teaching. According to Nagro (2020), this strategy can support students in building their own self-reflection skills. To do this, you could have them observe one another's teaching videos, or you can use lessons available online—we have found that YouTube offers a plethora of teaching videos, some better than others.

In Textbox 4.1, we offer a list of questions that can be used when teacher candidates watch a video recording of their own teaching. There are a handful of questions they should consider before viewing the observation, as well as questions to consider while they watch and after viewing the recording. There is nothing sacred or perfect about this list of questions, and we recommend that you adjust the list to meet the unique needs of your students and your program expectations. Just be sure, though, that you have students look for both strengths and areas for improvement in their teaching, as well as create follow-up plans based on what they observed. In addition, you may want to consider changing the list of questions as teacher candidates progress through your program. For their first field experience, you might want to focus on just a few questions (such as having students identify their biggest strengths and weaknesses) and add additional questions for reflection in later semesters.

Textbox 4.1

Questions for Teacher Candidate Reflection on Teaching

Questions to Ask Before They Watch the Video Recording

1. What was the learning objective of the lesson I was teaching?
2. Based on my lesson assessment, what percentage of students met that learning objective?
3. Based on my lesson assessment, what percentage of students did not meet the learning objective?
4. What clues do I have as to why those students did not meet the learning objective?
5. What went well in my lesson?
6. What did not go well in my lesson?

Questions to Ask After They Watch the Video Recording

1. What are the top three things I observed myself doing well in this video?
2. What are the top three things I observed myself doing in this video that could be improved?
3. What did I notice when viewing the video that I had not observed when I taught the lesson?
4. Based on what I noticed, what adjustments should I make to my teaching for these students in the future?
5. What else should I think about or note for myself?
6. What questions do I have for my school-based cooperating teacher, my university supervisor, or my professors after viewing myself teach?

We also suggest that if there is a specific mannerism or word the teacher candidate uses frequently, the university supervisor might consider asking them to tally their use of it when watching the video. For example, Marla has noticed that many of her students say phrases such as "um" or "you know" very frequently in their lessons (and, if she is honest, she uses "um" and "y'all" a lot herself). In some cases, the use of these phrases is distracting in the classroom, thus impacting students' ability to effectively teach the lesson. For these students, the teacher asks them to tally the number of times they say "um" in the lesson and then reflect on how to reduce that number. After their next recorded lesson, she asks them to tally again to see if it is reduced by simply being aware of it. In Marla's experience, student awareness has always reduced the instances of the distracting phrase. A similar strategy could be used for teacher candidates who tend to remain in the same part of the classroom for most of their instruction—they can be asked to record how long they spend in each quadrant of the classroom.

2 Clear Expectations for Students

Our second recommendation for remote field experience observations is to clearly communicate expectations for students, regarding both technology requirements and teaching performance. When students know what to expect, they are more likely to be successful. Textbox 4.2 shows an example of clearly articulated instructions used to ensure there is not a mismatch between faculty expectations and students' understandings of those expectations (Schaelling, 2018). In addition to the assignment instructions, we also suggest having a clear grading rubric for the observations and providing this to the students before they begin planning their lessons. When students use rubrics for assignment completion, their quality of work improves (Panadero & Romero, 2014; Panadero et al., 2023). We discuss rubrics in more detail in Chapter 6. Besides providing students with clear written instructions, you may find that providing students with step-by-step videos may also be helpful. This could include videos on how to use specific technologies, how to change video formats or compress videos, how to upload videos for submission, and even how to set up their camera to record.

Textbox 4.2

Sample Expectations for Students

Dear Students,

Congratulations on reaching this point in your degree program. This semester, you will be participating in a field placement and will be remotely observed. Below, you will find the information you will need for these observations:

Technology Requirements

1. **External Webcam with Wide-Angle Lens**—your tablet or smartphone likely has a high-quality camera, but in order to complete the requirements for observations, you will need a camera that has both a wide-angle lens and a high-quality microphone to pick up all sound in the classroom. This tool will be used in tandem with your computer or mobile device for recording the lesson.

2. **Flexible Gooseneck**—this tool is used to hold your camera in place during observations and reduce the likelihood of students knocking over the camera. Alternatively, you can select to have another adult sit with the camera during your lesson.

Observation Protocol

1. Identify the lesson you will teach for your observation. Your selected lesson should be approximately 30–45 minutes in length, so plan accordingly. If you teach longer class sessions (e.g., a 1-hour mathematics class), you do not need to record the entire student independent work time.

2. Send your completed lesson plan, using the university lesson plan template, to your university supervisor at least 96 hours before you plan to teach the lesson.

3. Your university supervisor will return your lesson plan to you, with explicit feedback, within 48 hours. Use that feedback to update your lesson plan.

> **Textbox 4.2 (Continued)**
>
> 4. On the day you will teach the lesson, set up the camera in your classroom. Be sure that the camera is placed in a location that has a clear view of the entire classroom and where there is no distracting noise (e.g., a fan next to it) that will prevent the classroom sounds from being heard.
> 5. Before teaching your lesson, start the recording. Be sure to record your lesson directly to your computer or mobile device.
> 6. During your planning time or that evening, preview the video to ensure the camera is facing the correct direction and the sound is working.
> 7. Respond to the lesson reflection questions assigned.
> 8. Upload both your lesson video recording and your reflection question responses to the course learning management system (LMS).

3 Creating Clear Guidelines for Faculty, Cooperating Teachers, and Host Schools

It is not just the students who will need clear guidance when it comes to remote observations. We want to ensure that the faculty, cooperating teachers, and host schools are all on the same page when it comes to working with the student(s). Gorni et al. (2024) report that clear guidelines for both students and faculty had a significant impact on the quality of remote observations for field experiences among physical education teacher candidates. Currin et al. (2019) report that some university supervisors report concerns about implementing remote observation protocols and procedures that they did not get the opportunity to help design. With this in mind, we highly recommend including both experienced and newer university supervisors in the development of the guidelines, as well as seeking ongoing feedback from them regarding how the protocol is working for both students and themselves. Additionally, in Marla's experience, it is important that training occurs for all faculty who will engage in the remote observation, the same as what would be expected in a face-to-face observation. Additional training may need to occur for the faculty related to technology and ways they can help their students.

It is also critical that you communicate to host schools and cooperating teachers the expectations surrounding the video recordings. Marla's university has been doing remote field experience observations for about ten years. Pre-COVID, they found that some schools and districts were hesitant to allow video recording in their schools. However, since 2020 they have noticed that schools are more willing to allow remote observations, as long as a clear process is in place and communicated to the school. In fact, they have found that some schools prefer remote observation because it reduces the number of people entering and exiting the school, which helps with school safety concerns. They do, however, frequently run into challenges with school district firewalls that block the use of certain video platforms. In these situations, the university and host school work together to develop a solution that works within the school's parameters, meets the observation requirements, and protects the confidentiality of all PK–12 students in the classroom. Textbox 4.3 offers a sample letter to a school district outlining the video observation protocol—depending on the school and district, this approval may need to come from a school district central office instead of from an individual principal. Please note that the letter is relatively short and does not provide every detail of the protocol—this is intentional, as we know that school administrators have multiple demands on their time and often appreciate succinct communications. We would suggest that you also create a more in-depth explanation of your video observation process, possibly in the form of a FAQ sheet, to provide to schools and districts who request additional information.

> **Textbox 4.3**
>
> ## Sample Letter to School District
>
> Dear Principal,
>
> Thank you for partnering with us in supporting the five teacher candidates planning to do their field placements in your school this semester.
>
> This letter is to inform you of our remote field experience observation protocol.
>
> 1. All teacher candidates will be observed using an asynchronous video-based observation.
> 2. Teacher candidates will use a Swivl C Series Robot to video record their lessons.
> 3. After recording the lesson, the teacher candidate will upload the video into the VoiceThread video platform.
> 4. The teacher candidate will view the video and self-reflect on his/her teaching using the Imaginary University lesson reflection form.
> 5. The teacher candidate will share the unique login information for accessing the video with their university supervisor. The login information will only be shared with the university supervisor, and will not be accessible to other university faculty members or other students.
> 6. The university supervisor will watch the video recording, offering feedback to the teacher candidate.
> 7. The teacher candidate will watch the video a second time, taking the feedback into consideration.
> 8. The teacher candidate will respond to the university supervisor feedback after viewing the video.
>
> *(Continued)*

> **Textbox 4.3 (Continued)**
>
> **9** The back-and-forth interactions between the teacher candidate and the university supervisor will continue until the lesson observation is fully discussed and analyzed.
>
> **10** The video will be deleted.
>
> Because the teacher candidate and the university supervisor are the only individuals who will have access to view the video, the privacy of individual students in your school can be protected.
>
> Because the university supervisor is watching these videos and does have access to confidential student information, he/she undergoes a yearly state-approved background check and annual training on FERPA and other legal requirements surrounding schools.
>
> Feel free to contact us at FieldExperience@imaginaryuniversity.edu with any questions or concerns you may have.
>
> Sincerely,
>
> Dr. Sarah Smith
>
> Director of Field Experiences, Imaginary University
>
> Please indicate below whether you consent to the use of remote observations in your school.
>
> I consent to the use of remote observations in my school. _____
>
> I do not consent to the use of remote observations in my school. _____
>
> Signature _____

Avoid This

While it is important to be proactive and tell teachers what *to* do, we also want to provide you with information on things we suggest you should *not* do. Below is a list of things we have personally done or seen/heard other instructors do that they have learned is not all that effective when it comes to remote observations.

1 Being unprepared for technology challenges

The reality is that technological challenges will occasionally occur anytime we use technology for instruction. We simply cannot expect that our technology tools will work perfectly all of the time. So, we need to be prepared for technology issues that will arise. At this point, we also want to remind you that unexpected glitches impacting the observation are not unique to remote observation. Some common challenges for face-to-face observations include fire drills, absent students, and unexpected assemblies or other school events.

The most common technology issue we see is spotty internet that makes it challenging, or even impossible, to have a consistent connection to the video platform, especially when synchronous observations are occurring. We have two suggestions for proactively preparing for this, but you will likely devise your own solutions to this challenge. First, students can be directed to use a mobile hotspot (or their phone as a hotspot) if the school internet has a tendency to be unpredictable—this only works if the cell coverage in the area is reliable. Secondly, students can do asynchronous observations that they record directly onto a device and then later upload to the video software. This solution is time consuming for students, due to upload times, but may be more reliable.

A second concern that arises in remote video-based observation is that the camera may not have a wide enough angle to view all students in the classroom, thus missing some of the students and interactions that take place (O'Neil et al., 2017). To proactively reduce this challenge, we recommend that all students be directed to use cameras with wide-angle lenses, as this will increase the percentage of the classroom that is visible in the video. Other common technology issues include poor sound, which prevents the university faculty member from hearing the teacher candidate and the PK–12 students, or the webcam accidentally getting knocked over or moved during the observation. We suggest purchasing a basic external microphone and testing it before the observations. And some teacher candidates have found that asking a trusted adult in their building to sit next to the camera can prevent its movement.

2 Not getting consent from school and district personnel for video-based observations

We mentioned in the previous section that it is imperative for teacher educators to communicate remote observation expectations to host schools. But, before doing that, you also need to ensure the host schools understand that observations will be remote and that students and teachers will be video recorded. We suggest getting written permission for these video observations from school and district administration. Because this can be a timely endeavor, especially when working with larger school districts, you will need to begin this process well in advance of the beginning of the semester. If you have not worked with the host district previously, you should expect a lot of questions during this phase of the process, but those questions may be reduced if you have a good FAQ sheet to share outlining the video protocol and protections that are in place for all people in the classroom.

3 Not explicitly training university faculty on supervision strategies and the use of technology tools

The reality is that not all university supervisors know how to use effective supervision techniques (Capello, 2020; Ubogu, 2024), and many don't have the skills needed to implement remote observation (MacMath & DeGagne, 2023). This means that explicit training is needed for all university personnel supporting remote observation. Training faculty is similar to offering instruction to any group of learners—you must include opportunities for instruction, practicing together, and independent practice paired with explicit and frequent feedback (Archer & Hughes, 2011). When university faculty receive training on remote observations, their scoring of observed lessons will be consistent from one faculty member to another (Johnson et al., 2022), ensuring that all teacher candidates receive similar expectations and grading experiences.

Let's Practice—"We Do"

Professor Ruiz oversees all field experiences for teacher candidates at her university, which is located in a state with many rural communities that are a significant distance from the university. In the past, Professor Ruiz and her colleagues have done all observations in person. Due to the travel time to get to each teacher candidate's placement school and the costs associated with travel, they were only able to observe each candidate twice per semester. Professor Ruiz knows that additional feedback and observation will support the teacher candidates in growing their instructional and classroom management skills. For the upcoming semester, she is planning to do one in-person and three remote observations of each student, doubling the number of observations she was previously able to do. Because this will be a new process for her university and for their partner school districts, she wants to ensure that she has clearly outlined how things will work.

Now it is time to practice. This is the "We Do" part of good teaching. Answer the questions in Textbox 4.4 using the blank spaces provided. Once

---

Textbox 4.4

1. Help Professor Ruiz write a letter to the host schools explaining the new observation protocol, with a specific explanation of why the protocol is changing.

2. Identify which of the four observations will be in person and which three observations will be remote. Offer a rationale for your decision.

3. Identify the responsibilities of each party (Professor Ruiz, university supervisor, host school, and teacher candidate) in the remote observation process.

(Continued)

> **Textbox 4.4 (Continued)**
>
> 4 Select one challenge that Professor Ruiz may encounter while implementing this new protocol and develop a plan for proactively preventing that challenge.

you have your answers, share them on social media using the hashtag #OnlineTeacherPrep and tagging both of us in your post. You may also take a look at the suggestions included in Appendix A if you get stumped (or need a little validation that you know what you are doing).

Apply to Your Own Courses—"You Do"

It is now your time to practice creating a plan for remote field experience observation in your own online course. Complete the tasks listed in Textbox 4.5. Please note that this is a long list of tasks, most of which are very time consuming. Don't expect to do this "You Do" in a few minutes—it will likely take several hours. You may also choose to complete the questions that are most relevant to your current university needs.

> **Textbox 4.5**
>
> 1 In 1–2 paragraphs, explain why you are interested in doing video-based teacher candidate observations.

Textbox 4.5 (Continued)

2 Describe the benefits to your current observation protocol.

3 Describe the drawbacks and challenges to your current observation protocol.

4 Describe how the use of remote observations will help to reduce the drawbacks and challenges noted in question 3 (if it will reduce them).

5 Describe the challenges you anticipate having with remote field experience observations.

6 Make a list of the resources your teacher education program has available to support this endeavor. Remember that resources may include people, expertise, finances, technology tools, or other physical items.

(Continued)

> **Textbox 4.5 (Continued)**
>
> **7** Identify which faculty members will serve as university supervisors for remote observations.
>
> **8** Make a plan for how those university supervisors will receive training on effective remote observations and the related technology tools.
>
> **9** Create a detailed timeline for the launch and ongoing support of remote observations.
>
> **Congratulations!**—You have begun thinking about ways to use remote observations in your program or your online class!

References

Altalhab, S., Alsuhaibani, Y., & Gillies, D. (2020). The reflective diary experiences of EFL pre-service teachers. *Reflective Practice, 22*(2), 173–186. https://doi.org/10.1080/14623943.2020.1865903

Archer, A. L., & Hughes, C. A. (2011). *Explicit instruction: Effective and efficient teaching.* Guilford Press.

Ault, M. J., Spriggs, A. D., Bausch, M. E., & Courtade, G. R. (2019). Evaluation of remote versus face-to-face observation of teacher candidates in an alternative certification program. *Rural Special Education Quarterly, 38*(3), 124–136. https://doi.org/10.1177/875687051986103

Black, G. L. (2015). Developing teacher candidates' self-efficacy through reflection and supervising teacher support. *In Education, 21*(1), 78–98. https://doi.org/10.37119/ojs2015.v21i1.171

Capello, S. (2020). Tensions in the preparation of university supervisors: Dual perspectives from supervisors and administrators. *Journal of Educational Supervision, 3*(1), 18–35. https://doi.org/10.31045/jes.3.1.3

Chilton, H., & McCracken, W. (2017). New technology, changing pedagogies? Exploring the concept of remote teaching placement supervision. *Higher Education Pedagogies, 2*(1), 116–130. https://doi.org/10.1080/23752696.2017.1366276

Cohen, J., Wong, V., Krishnamachari, A., & Berlin, R. (2020). Teacher coaching in a simulated environment. *Educational Evaluation and Policy Analysis, 42*(2), 208–231. https://doi.org/10.3102/0162373720906217

Crawford, A., Varghese, C., Hsu, H.-Y., Zucker, T., Landry, S., Assel, M., Monsegue-Bailey, P., & Bhavsar, V. (2021). A comparative analysis of instructional coaching approaches: Face-to-face versus remote coaching in preschool classrooms. *Journal of Educational Psychology, 113*(8), 1609–1627. https://doi.org/10.1037/edu0000691

Currin, E., Schroeder, S., Bondy, E., & Castanheira, B. (2019). Tinker, tailor, supervisor, spy: Lessons learned from distant supervision. *Journal of Educational Supervision, 2*(1), 78–97. https://doi.org/10.31045/jes.2.1.5

Dalinger, T., Thomas, K. B., Stansberry, S., & Xiu, Y. (2020). A mixed reality simulation offers strategic practice for pre-service teachers. *Computers and Education, 144,* 103696. https://doi.org/10.1016/j.compedu.2019.103696

Dieker, L. A., Hynes, M. C., Hughes, C. E., Hardin, S., & Becht, K. (2015). TLE TeachLivE™: Using technology to provide quality professional development in rural schools. *Rural Special Education Quarterly, 34*(3), 11–16. https://doi.org/10.1177/875687051503400303

Ersozlu, Z., Ledger, S., Ersozlu, A., Mayne, F., & Wildy, H. (2021). Mixed-reality learning environments in teacher education: An analysis of TeachLivE™ research. *Sage Open, 11*(3). https://doi.org/10.1177/21582440211032155

Gorni, R. L., Nurdin, D., & Komariah, A. (2024). Leveraging technology for remote supervision: Overcoming challenges in supervising geographically dispersed student teachers. *International Journal of Educational Qualitative Quantitative Research, 3*(1), 9–20. https://doi.org/10.58418/ijeqqr.v3i1.95

Gray, L., and Lewis, L. (2021). *Use of Educational Technology for Instruction in Public Schools: 2019–20 (NCES 2021-017)*. U.S. Department of Education. Washington, DC:

National Center for Education Statistics. https://nces.ed.gov/pubsearch/pubsinfo.asp?pubid=2021017.

Hoch, E., Scheiter, K., & Sassenberg, K. (2024). Promotion focus, but not prevention focus of teachers and students matters when shifting towards technology-based instruction in schools. *Scientific Reports, 14*(1), 1–12.

Horn, A. L., Rock, M. L., Chezan, L. C., Bobzien, J. L., Karadimou, O., & Alturki, A. (2023). Effects of ecoaching on the occurrence, equity, and variety of behavior specific praise during Mursion™ simulations. *Journal of Special Education Technology, 38*(4), 501–514. https://doi.org/10.1177/01626434231152893

Johnson, E. S., Zheng, Y., Crawford, A. R., & Moylan, L. A. (2022). Evaluating an explicit instruction teacher observation protocol through a validity argument approach. *Journal of Experimental Education, 90*(2), 419–434.

Kheirzadeh, S., & Sistani, N. (2018). The effect of reflective teaching on Iranian EFL students' achievement: The case of teaching experience and level of education. *Australian Journal of Teacher Education, 43*(2), 143–156.

Kraft, M. A., Blazar, D., & Hogan, D. (2018). The effect of teacher coaching on instruction and achievement: A meta-analysis of the causal evidence. *Review of Educational Research, 88*(4), 547–588. https://doi.org/10.3102/0034654318759268

Liang, J. (2015). Live video classroom observation: An effective approach to reducing reactivity in collecting observational information for teacher professional development. *Journal of Education for Teaching, 41*(3), 235–253. https://doi.org/10.1080/02607476.2015.1045314

Mac Mahon, B., Ó Grádaigh, S., & Ní Ghuidhir, S. (2019). Super vision: The role of remote observation in the professional learning of student teachers and novice placement tutors. *TechTrends, 63*, 703–710. https://doi.org/10.1007/s11528-019-00432-z

MacMath, S., & DeGagne, D. (2023). Learning from faculty mentors who had to mentor and evaluate teacher candidates completing a remote practicum in the early stages of the COVID-19 pandemic in Canada. *Journal of Educational Supervision, 6*(3). https://doi.org/10.31045/jes.6.3.4

Miller, L. S. (2023). Supervision to support reflective practices. *Journal of Educational Supervision, 6*(1). https://doi.org/10.31045/jes.6.1.1

Moayeri, M., & Rahimiy, R. (2019). The significance of promoting teacher reflection: A review article. *Latin American Journal of Content & Language Integrated Learning, 12*(1). https://doi.org/10.5294/laclil.2019.12.1.6

Nagro, S. A. (2020). Reflecting on others before reflecting on self: Using video evidence to guide teacher candidates' reflective practices. *Journal of Teacher Education, 71*(4), 420–433. https://doi.org/10.1177/0022487119872700

O'Neil, K., Krause, J. M., & Douglas, S. (2017). University supervisor perceptions of live remote supervision in physical education teacher education. *International*

Journal of Kinesiology in Higher Education, 1(4), 113–125. https://doi.org/10.1080/24711616.2017.1328190

Onyett, L. (2011). A system for the remote observation of student teachers. In M. Koehler & P. Mishra (Eds.), *Proceedings of SITE 2011–Society for Information Technology & Teacher Education International Conference* (pp. 599–601). Association for the Advancement of Computing in Education (AACE). https://www.learntechlib.org/primary/p/36337/

Panadero, E., Jonsson, A., Pinedo, L., & Fernández-Castilla, B. (2023). Effects of rubrics on academic performance, self-regulated learning, and self-efficacy: A meta-analytic review. *Educational Psychology Review, 35*, Article 113. https://doi.org/10.1007/s10648-023-09823-4

Panadero, E., & Romero, M. (2014). To rubric or not to rubric? The effects of self-assessment on self-regulation, performance and self-efficacy. *Assessment in Education: Principles, Policy & Practice, 21*(2), 133–148. https://doi.org/10.1080/0969594X.2013.877872

Schaelling, C. (2018). "Does that make sense?" The importance of clear assignment instructions and rubrics. *Writing Center Analysis Papers*, Paper 23. https://digitalcommons.usu.edu/wc_analysis/23

Slade, M. L., Burnham, T. J., Catalana, S. M., & Waters, T. (2019). The impact of reflective practice on teacher candidates' learning. *International Journal for the Scholarship of Teaching and Learning, 13*(2), Article 15. https://doi.org/10.20429/ijsotl.2019.130215

Ubogu, R. (2024). Supervision of instruction: A strategy for strengthening teacher quality in secondary school education. *International Journal of Leadership in Education, 27*(1), 99–116. https://doi.org/10.1080/13603124.2020.1829711

United States Department of Education. (n.d.). *FAQs on photos and videos under FERPA*. https://studentprivacy.ed.gov/faq/faqs-photos-and-videos-under-ferpa

United States Department of Education. (2021). *A parent guide to the Family Education Rights and Privacy Act (FERPA)*. https://studentprivacy.ed.gov/sites/default/files/resource_document/file/A%20parent%20guide%20to%20ferpa_508.pdf

Van Boxtel, J. M. (2017). Seeing is believing: Innovating the clinical practice experience for education specialist teacher candidates with video-based remote supervision. *Rural Special Education Quarterly, 36*(4), 180–190. https://doi.org/10.1177/8756870517737313

Wake, D., Dailey, D., Cotabish, A., & Benson, T. (2017). The effects of virtual coaching on teacher candidates' perceptions and concerns regarding on-demand corrective feedback. *Journal of Technology and Teacher Education, 25*(3), 327–357. https://www.learntechlib.org/primary/p/173825/

5 Authentic Assessment as an Instructional Practice

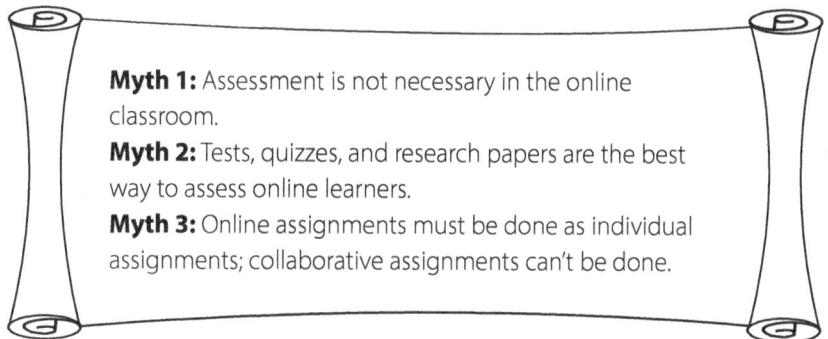

Myth 1: Assessment is not necessary in the online classroom.
Myth 2: Tests, quizzes, and research papers are the best way to assess online learners.
Myth 3: Online assignments must be done as individual assignments; collaborative assignments can't be done.

Debunking the Myths

The myths surrounding effective assessments, especially for online learning, are endless. Before we discuss the myths surrounding assessments, we want to identify the role and importance of assessment in learning. We realize that the readers of this book are likely all education faculty (or aspiring education faculty) and have extensive knowledge about student assessments. In fact, there are likely some readers who know significantly more about assessing student learning than we do! But we want to ensure that we are all on the same page about the role of assessments before we proceed. The reality is that good assessment, for students from preschool through graduate school, supports and guides student learning (Gallagher et al., 2024; Ibarra-Saiz et al., 2021; Murdoch et al., 2024).

University faculty should utilize a combination of both formative and summative assessments throughout their coursework. Formative assessments can be defined as those assessments that are used throughout a course or learning unit in order to evaluate student learning, offer feedback to students, and adjust the instruction to ensure students meet the learning outcomes (Carney et al., 2022). Conversely, summative assessments are used to assess student learning at the end of a course or learning unit (Kibble, 2017). We want to note that, in the higher education classroom, summative student assessments and overall program assessments related to program learning outcomes (PLOs) are generally required by the regional accrediting body (Carney et al., 2022; Krzykowski & Kinser, 2014), so they must be included in some of your courses.

Now that we have discussed the purpose of assessments, let's dig into the meat of this topic by exploring the myths. The first myth we have encountered from colleagues is that assessment is simply not necessary if our courses are well designed. In truth, we tend to hear this more from our colleagues outside the field of education, but we have heard it from some education professors as well. This myth is simply not true and can have negative impacts both for student learning and for the university.

For practical purposes, assessment is mandatory for universities. Student assessments in the higher education classroom are used to evaluate student mastery of the student learning objectives (SLOs) for the specific course (McClendon & Ho, 2016), which may or may not be aligned with state standards for teacher education. Mathers et al. (2018) report that university faculty believe that student learning should be enhanced through the completion of coursework; but this is not always the case, and some students do not grow in their knowledge of a specific subject area simply by taking a college class. The results from student assessments can be used to support faculty in modifying and adapting the instruction provided to ensure that all learners meet the outlined SLOs and grow in their knowledge of the subject matter being taught (Manis et al., 2022; Mathers et al., 2018; McClendon & Ho, 2016).

In addition to its use for accreditation purposes, assessment is used in higher education classrooms to evaluate how learning is going and make timely adjustments as needed to support students (Manis et al., 2022). A good assessment process involves work for both the teacher and the student and offers valuable information to both about student learning and student areas for additional instruction and practice (Romero & Gonzalez, 2023). The use of assessments, both formative and summative, is a vital part of the learning process and supports both the learner and the teacher in determining how to proceed in the process (Shepard, 2000).

The second myth we want to debunk is that tests and research papers are the only way to assess online learners. In our experience, many faculty rely on online exams to assess learning in the virtual classroom. While this can be "easy," we recommend finding alternative ways to assess student knowledge, with a focus on using assessment tools that align with the higher levels of learning in Bloom's taxonomy (since you are all teachers, we are not going to describe this framework to you, but we do recommend you take a moment to refresh yourself on its use). When you give a test, it will likely automatically be graded by your learning management system (LMS), making grading a breeze. In our busy faculty schedules, we know that it can be challenging to find time to grade student work, especially when you have a heavy teaching load (so we understand the appeal!). And we are seeing an increasing number of online learning tools that have the capability to incorporate quiz questions right into the reading and viewing assignments.

But the use of formalized tests does not necessarily accurately reflect student knowledge of the course content. When students are assessed using traditional tests, they are not asked to demonstrate higher-level understanding of the concepts or critical thinking skills, but instead are simply required to regurgitate basic information (Azim & Khan, 2012). Wiggins (1990) argued that the use of traditional tests and quizzes to assess learning encourages students to cram and memorize the information just to pass the test, but then quickly forget what they learned.

In our experience, though the use of tests and quizzes should not be the primary assessment tool in your coursework, it can be beneficial when we need to assess basic student understanding of a concept. These assessment tools can be effectively used for information that has a clear right answer and requires students to memorize content. For example, Marla uses a quiz to assess student knowledge of basic special education terms (e.g., Free Appropriate Public Education, Individualized Education Program, inclusion, etc.). Each of these terms has a definition, and she uses a quiz in which students match the term to the definition. But the use of a quiz or test would not be appropriate for evaluating whether students are able to write an individualized education program (IEP) or lesson plan. In Kathy's undergraduate courses, she uses quizzes as a form of reading checks to ensure that students are completing the required textbook readings for the week. These quizzes are only worth a few points, but they do motivate students to read the textbook, which we find that many students consistently do not do. We suggest that you use tests and quizzes when appropriate, but do not rely on them as your primary assessment tool.

A third myth that is important to discuss in this chapter is that collaborative assignments cannot be done and that online assignments must be completed individually. This is definitely not the case, at least in our experience. And always relying on independent work does not accurately reflect our students' future career expectations. The reality is that students will be teaming up with colleagues, families, and community members as they support student learning in their schools. While teachers may teach in their classrooms alone, they do not work alone. Good teaching is a collaborative process, and we need to prepare students for working together. Learning to work collaboratively with other school professionals is a key skill that your students need to understand, and by collaborating online, they are able to learn skills they can take to their own jobs and use when their "team" cannot meet at the same time or place.

There are a variety of ways online instructors can incorporate collaborative assessment into their courses. They can utilize group projects, especially projects that reflect real-world situations that teachers encounter in schools, like designing a grade-level scope and sequence or preparing for a mock IEP meeting. Altinay (2016) reports that the use of collaborative assessment supports students in being self-reflective learners and increases assessment skills. When using group projects, though, faculty must be intentional in planning and should allow groups sufficient time to work together, expect each group to create group norms and expectations for collaboration, offer opportunities for each group member to evaluate one another and themselves, and regularly monitor group progress (Scherling, 2011). As educators (or future educators), our students need to have the skills required to assess learning, so this strategy offers them the opportunity to practice this skill. It is important to note, though, that if you have students assess one another's work, you must explicitly teach them how to do so and create classroom norms around respectful assessment (McConnell, 2002).

As you consider using group projects in your coursework, though, you must be aware of, and prepare for, the potential challenges that may arise. Hilliard et al. (2020) report that online group projects can cause anxiety for many students, but the use of group guidelines and teamwork strategies reduces the anxiety for the majority of learners. Additionally, online instructors might consider having students assess one another's assignment submissions. This strategy can reduce the faculty workload and help students learn the necessary skills to evaluate their own work, as well as the work of others (McConnell, 2002). Students also report that challenges may arise with accountability for group members (Bakir et al., 2020). We recommend regular check-ins with each group and anonymous evaluations of group members at the end of each project. Finally, in our experience, online group projects in asynchronous courses can be a bit challenging, as students may need to identify common times for meetings. Some students may be resistant to these as they intentionally selected asynchronous courses due to scheduling demands. If this is the case, we have found it to be beneficial to remind students that group meetings can occur at any time (and some groups will meet at 2 a.m.!) and offer solutions for asynchronous collaboration when a common meeting time cannot be identified.

One way to overcome the idea that collaborative assignments are not possible is by creating opportunities for your students to build community in your classroom (see Chapter 1). Another way you can overcome this myth is to have a rubric or questionnaire in place where students grade each other's participation. While it is not foolproof, having conversations about responsibility and having them submit evaluations that the other members do not see have also been known to work. Kathy has had several assignments in which students worked together to submit a final group project. In her experience, many students start out groaning about group work in the online environment, but by the end of the class many mention that it was better than they thought it would be.

Tools to Use—"I Do"

In the Introduction, we briefly mentioned the Universal Design for Learning (UDL) framework and discuss it more thoroughly in Appendix D. If you have not noticed, we are huge advocates of this teaching framework and try to design our own instruction with UDL in mind. By designing high-quality assessments, we are meeting all three UDL principles—multiple means of representation, multiple means of engagement, and multiple means of action and expression. This is one of the many reasons we felt this chapter was so important to include in a book about designing quality online classrooms.

Below are several ways we try to incorporate authentic assessment into our online courses.

You may have figured out by now that we are not instructors who usually give tests or have students write long research papers. We don't do this for two reasons. First, we have learned that these forms of assessment are not good evaluations of student learning. And, secondly, tests and long papers can be tedious to grade—when you have a very high teaching load, you spend a lot of time grading! We do know that it may seem selfish to consider our own grading time when selecting assessments, but we also know that it matters—there are only twenty-four hours in the day, and we cannot (nor should we) spend all of that time working. We need to use the time we have wisely. We try our best, when possible, to create assessments that reflect the skills our students will need in their own PK–12 classrooms, today or in the future.

As much as possible, we look for authentic assessments that align with course contents. Authentic assessment in the higher education setting often involves tasks that mimic what students will be required to do in their jobs (Ajjawi et al., 2024). There is evidence that the rates of students cheating are reduced when faculty use authentic assessments in lieu of more traditional assessment methods (Ellis et al., 2020). We also share in Chapter 3 how we utilize authentic assessments in asynchronous discussions.

1 Creating Professional Developments for Colleagues

One way we incorporate authenticity into our coursework is by having students complete professional development projects. In this type of activity, students create a visual through some presentation software program such as Prezi, Google Slides, Canva, or PowerPoint. Students put the required information into their presentation and then record themselves giving a presentation. We offer choices to record themselves through tools such as Zoom, Yuja, and ScreenPal. The professional development type of assignment allows students to work on presentation skills, as well as learn how to be succinct in their speaking, as usually we give them time limits. In her Special Education Teaching Methods course, Marla asks students to create a ten-minute webinar that could be used to teach colleagues about one evidence-based inclusion strategy. In those ten minutes, students must describe the research supporting the specific intervention and explain how it could be implemented in their school. A few of Marla's students have been asked to give these presentations to their colleagues during a faculty meeting. Kathy also uses this type of authentic assessment as a way to build the skills they will need as teachers. Kathy has heard from students that they have been able to use the presentations they created (without the video) for job interviews (in which they got the job!) or even for teacher training. These stories are what we mean when we talk about creating assessments that are user friendly and something your students can use in their everyday lives. Textbox 5.1 provides an example of a professional development project for a graduate class where students are asked to briefly review assistive and instructional technologies that can be used in the classroom. Because this is a special education graduate course, they are asked to address assistive technology in a student's IEP. You will also notice that artificial intelligence was used to assist in creating this project and that the AI was even given credit. For more information on AI, see Appendix F.

Textbox 5.1

Technology Project

Instructions: This week you have read about using instructional and assistive technologies in the classroom. You have learned more about using instructional technology in the classroom and have begun identifying technologies you can incorporate into your classroom. You have also spent time learning about the importance of integrating assistive technology (AT) into the classroom and how to document the use of AT into a student's individualized education program (IEP).

One way to meet the diverse needs in your classroom is by integrating these technologies into your planning, delivery, and assessment of learners. This week you will be required to create a professional development presentation that you would give to other teachers in your school.

Your presentation should be at least 20–30 minutes. You will need to create your presentation in a software program such as PowerPoint,

(Continued)

Textbox 5.1 (Continued)

Canva, or Prezi. You will then need to record yourself presenting to your colleagues (you do not have to actually give the presentation). Recordings should be made through Yuja, ScreenPal, or Zoom. References and citations must be included. You may either cite in your slides and then create a reference slide at the end, or if you are only using one reference in a slide, you may include a footnote. Choose one of these ways; do not use both.

When submitting, make sure you submit *both* the actual presentation and also a link to the recording. Make sure to review your rubric so you know how you will be graded.

Credit for pieces of the project below is given to Microsoft Gemini (AI). The content components below include excerpts from responses given by AI and have been reworded to work for the course.

Your presentation will need to include the following elements:

Title: Name your presentation—be creative. Make sure you also include your name on the slide.

Definition/Purpose:

- Define assistive technology (AT) and provide examples of AT tools used in education.
- Define instructional technology (IT) and provide examples of IT tools used in education.
- How does the intended purpose of each type of technology differ?

Benefits and Applications:

- Discuss the benefits of AT for students with specific learning needs (e.g., dyslexia, visual impairments, attention deficit hyperactivity disorder [ADHD]).
- How can IT be used to enhance the learning experience for all students, regardless of ability?
- Share specific examples of how AT and IT can be used together to create a more inclusive learning environment.

> **Textbox 5.1 (Continued)**
>
> **Assistive Technology in the IEP:**
> - This is where you need to discuss addressing AT in the IEP.
> - Think about what AT is used for, when and how it will be used, as well as information on training students, parents, and educators for using the AT.
>
> **Considerations and Challenges:**
> - What are some challenges educators might face when implementing AT and IT in the classroom (e.g., accessibility, cost, training)?
> - How can we ensure equitable access to technology for all students?

2 Role Plays

A second strategy we recommend for assessing student learning is the use of role plays. The use of role plays allows students the opportunity to practice the skills they are learning and receive feedback on those skills before they are asked to use those skills in the workplace (Flaherty, 2023). Students report appreciating the opportunity to use role play to practice and improve skills in a safe space where they will receive constructive feedback to support their individual growth (Allemang et al., 2022; Ng et al., 2023).

In the online classroom, there are a few ways that faculty can use role plays for assessment. First, you can use traditional role plays in which all students are in the same "space" at the same time, acting out a scenario. If you host synchronous class sessions, we have found this to be a good strategy for supporting student learning. In larger classes, we suggest using breakout rooms for small groups to role-play scenarios such as teaching a lesson, with their classmates serving as the students; parent-teacher conferences; and IEP meetings. Secondly, you as the course instructor can do 1:1 role plays with students to help them refine certain skills. This can be time consuming, though, as you will need to schedule individual time with each student to accomplish this task. Marla has used this to support students who request help preparing for parent-teacher conferences, especially when they anticipate a hard conversation with the parents or caregivers. While this was not used as a grade-based assessment for her students, Marla does offer informal feedback and continues practicing the parent-teacher conference with the student until both she and the student feel that the student is prepared to meet with the parents. Finally, the use of mixed-reality simulations can be used to role-play classroom and school-based scenarios, especially teaching situations. Mixed-reality simulations are technology-based experiences in which students practice situations that arise in the classroom; both the student and the live interactors involved in the simulation use avatars to interact in the virtual space (Budin, 2024). The use of mixed-reality simulations may improve teachers' lesson-planning skills (Driver et al., 2024) and support teacher candidates' skill development because they are able to practice the same skill as many times as necessary to master that skill (Aguilar & Flores, 2022; Carisma & Marais 2023). We do want to acknowledge that the cost for mixed-reality simulations is cost prohibitive for many teacher education programs.

3 Action Research

Finally, both of us also teach a class on action research. Action research is a process in which students identify a learning or behavior challenge in their classroom, take baseline data regarding the challenge, identify and implement a research-based intervention, evaluate the impact of that intervention, and make changes accordingly (Lohmann, 2023). The use of action research is a good summative assessment to evaluate our students' knowledge of all PLOs at the end of their teacher education program. Marla's action research project is broken down into two courses—in the first course, students identify the challenge, take baseline data, and design the intervention plan. In the second course, students implement the interventions they designed and evaluate the effectiveness of that specific intervention for the particular student or group of students. Kathy only teaches the course in one seven-week course, so her students do not implement the identified interventions. However, they walk through the steps of the action research and present their research to the class. Textbox 5.2 provides you with the directions for Kathy's assignment. If you look closely at the textbox, you will see information about how Kathy provides ongoing feedback to use for students' final project. This is discussed more in Chapter 7. She also provides—not seen in the textbox example—a sample calendar to help keep students from getting behind. This is something she has found that many students like having for multi-step projects such as the one in Textbox 5.2.

Textbox 5.2

Action Research Project—No Intervention Implementation

Each week you have reviewed a step of the action research process. This project will give you a chance to actually practice most of the steps required for action research. Once you have completed your action research project, you will share it with the class. While I want this project to be as authentic as possible, you will not be conducting the actual intervention phase in your classroom due to the time restraints of this course that would artificially limit the length and intensity of the intervention. Instead of implementing your intervention, you will identify possible interventions and walk through the process of creating an intervention plan. When we grade your weekly assignments, we will provide feedback on your plan so you will know if you are on the right track to implement the intervention after the course ends. **Please use the permission slip found HERE to obtain permission from your building administrator to complete this project.** *If you are not currently working in a school, please just write on the permission slip that you are doing the alternative version of the project.* There are alternative directions in the sample calendar below for those who are not currently working in a school and need to make adjustments to your project. If you are not in a school and have an idea for an action research project that you would like to do instead of the alternative, please contact me to set up a time to discuss. I am open to anything that will help you in your current/future career.

Each week, part of your assignment will be to provide information regarding the steps you have completed on your action research project for feedback. More information on this can be found in your weekly assignments. Those who do not take advantage of this opportunity are usually at a disadvantage when it comes time to complete the final project and usually do not do well. I highly recommend turning in the requested parts and reviewing the feedback along the way to help when it comes time to turn in your paper. Reviewing the feedback *and* reviewing the rubric will be the most helpful things you can do to ensure you are including what you need to. Those who fail to do these two things usually do not do well on large projects such as this!

(Continued)

Textbox 5.2 (Continued)

Please read the guidelines below carefully to ensure you are covering all the areas and including everything that is requested. You will have approximately a week and a half at the end of the term to put your project together and finalize it for a grade.

Your final paper will need to include the following information:

- Background information on the problem and how/why action research can help with the area of concern. You also need to include classroom setting information—tell me about the classroom—grade, number of students, type of class, adult/student ratio, etc. This section should include your problem statement.
- Baseline data.
- Intervention design—what steps will you take to conduct your interventions?
- Information on evidence-based interventions.
- Data collection methods and rationale.
- Information on how you can include the evidence-based practices (EBPs) into your classroom.

Your final paper should be approximately 6–8 pages in length (not including the title page, reference page, and appendices) and should include at a minimum 5 peer-reviewed references. This length is approximate.

Your paper will need to adhere to APA, 7th ed., using Times New Roman 12-point font. You will need to include the following:

1 APA-formatted title page (page 1)

2 Introduction to the study, including background information (½–1 page)
   a **See rubric for more information.**

3 Mini literature review (approximately 3–5 pages)
   a Discuss the **research base** of the evidence-based interventions you identified.

Textbox 5.2 (Continued)

  b Identify a top-choice intervention you would implement and discuss why you chose the evidence-based practice/interventions you did.

4 Methods section (1–2 pages)
  a Choose one of the interventions discussed in the literature review. Discuss why you chose to use this EBP/intervention first. Also discuss the considerations in choosing your EBP. This will be written in paragraph form, but include information similar to Textbox 4.1 on pages 56–58 of your classroom textbook.

  b Discuss your intervention design—write out your specific steps to implementing the intervention. This is similar to Table 4.1 in the textbook.

5 Data collection section (1 page)
  a Discuss your baseline data—what kind of data you collected, etc. Include a graph of your baseline data as well as your data collection sheets.

  b Discuss future intervention data collection—tell me the who, what, when, where, and why of your intervention data; how will you know if your intervention is effective?

  c Your paper must include data collection sheets (completed if doing the regular version and blank if doing the alternate version of the assignment).

  d Data collection forms would be best added at the end as appendices, as well as any tables or charts from your data collection.

6 Conclusion (last page)
  a Tie it all together—what did you learn from this project, and how/why is it important to you as a teacher?

7 References (on a page by itself and the final page of your paper)

8 Appendix A—signed permission slip

Authentic Assessment Ideas

We have given you several ways you can incorporate more authentic assessments into your online courses, instead of depending on research papers and tests/exams. We specifically mentioned three strategies that we use in our courses, but we also use many other authentic assessments in our courses. Throughout the book we have given other examples, such as in Chapter 3, where we discuss different types of discussion formats. Below we wanted to provide you even more ways to incorporate authentic assessments into your online courses. We hope that you will find some of these useful. Table 5.1 provides examples of different types of authentic assessments, as well as examples of specific activities that we have used throughout our time teaching online. If you are curious about what some of these may look like in practice, or you need an example to get your juices flowing, then take a peek at Appendix B.

Table 5.1 Authentic Assessment Ideas

Assessment Name	Examples
Role plays	Mock classroom instruction Mock parent-teacher conferences Mock individualized education program (IEP) meetings Mock faculty meetings Mock evaluation meetings with principal Mock co-teaching planning meetings Mock grade-level or department meetings
Professional development presentation	Collaboration among general and special educators Reading or math interventions Working with ELL students Culturally responsive teaching
Newsletters	Welcome back to school Information on the beginning of a unit Get to Know the Teacher letter to parents Parent Guide to Phonics Tips for supporting your child at home with math fact fluency

Assessment Name	Examples
Classroom management system	Classroom expectations poster Classroom expectations matrix Consequences, including rewards and punishments, for classroom behavior Crisis management plan Welcome Back to School Newsletter with classroom management information Data-tracking sheet for challenging behavior
Individualized education program	Mock individualized education programs (IEPs) and/or individualized family and service plans (IFSPs) meetings Write sections of the IEP or IFSP
Data collection practice	Collect behavior data for functional behavioral assessments (FBAs) (for special educators) Collect behavior data to assist in the multi-tiered systems of support (MTSS) process (for general educators) Create data collection sheets (electronic or paper) for specific data Brainstorm a list of ways to collect formative and summative data
Lesson plans	Create a UDL-friendly lesson plan Create a culturally responsive lesson plan
Miscellaneous	Classroom website Resource guide Handbook Teacher blog for communicating with families and caregivers How-to guide

Avoid This

While it is important to be proactive and tell teachers what *to* do, we also want to give you some ideas to avoid. These are things we have personally done or seen/heard other instructors do that are not considered authentic assessments or are not effective when focusing on authentic assessments.

1 Relying on tests to assess student knowledge

While we know that with large courses and teaching online, tests are what many believe is the easiest way to ensure that students are learning and the quickest way to grade. We also know that many tests are just about what you have memorized. There are tests that many of you give that are more scenario based, and that is great, but why not try something different and meet the needs of the diverse student population in your courses? As teachers, we need to practice what we teach, and while there is a time and place for tests, try to use them only when there is no other option for students to demonstrate their knowledge.

2 Having students practice skills before they are ready

In this chapter, we talked about a variety of ways to assess student knowledge and skills, through both formative and summative assessments. We do want to caution instructors to be careful not to jump to summative assessments too quickly, especially when those summative assessments involve working with actual children and families. Marla once saw a Classroom Management course in which students were asked to conduct a functional behavioral assessment (FBA) and implement a behavior intervention plan (BIP) starting on day 1 of the course. This was the first behavior course any of the students had taken, and none of them had been taught how to collect data, identify evidence-based interventions, or implement interventions. The instructor's thinking was that students would simply learn about each of those things while doing them. And while discovery learning is popular in today's classroom, despite the research findings that it is less effective than explicit instruction and should be preceded by high-quality explicit instruction (e.g., Almeida et al., 2021; Ashman et al., 2020), we do not believe it is appropriate to use discovery learning to have teacher candidates learn skills while practicing with actual PK–12 students. Our students must be explicitly taught the skills with instruction, practice, and feedback to the point of mastery before we ask them to practice those skills with children. So, this is just a reminder to ensure that your students are ready for the assessment before asking them to demonstrate their skills in a real classroom or school.

3 Not giving clear guidelines

Finally, we highly recommend that you avoid using unclear guidelines and expectations when designing formative and summative assessments for a course. When students are unsure what they are being asked to do, they are more likely to struggle to meet the expectations. Textbox 5.3 offers an example of unclear guidelines for an assignment, while Textbox 5.4 includes clearer instructions for the same formative assessment.

Textbox 5.3

Example of Unclear Assignment Instructions

Over the past few weeks, we have been learning about trauma-informed instruction in the PK–12 classroom. To demonstrate your understanding of this concept and its application in your own classroom and school, create a 5-minute video that you can use to teach your classroom paraprofessional about trauma-informed instruction. Be sure to include references and personal applications.

Textbox 5.4

Example of Clear Assignment Instructions

Over the past few weeks, we have been learning about trauma-informed instruction in the PK–12 classroom. To demonstrate your understanding of this concept and its application in your own classroom and school, create a video that you can use to teach your classroom paraprofessional about trauma-informed instruction. Your video should:

1. Be 5–8 minutes in length—this is a short video, so you will need to focus on being succinct.
2. Speak directly to the paraprofessional, using his/her name as appropriate.
3. Provide a basic overview of the research about adverse childhood experiences (ACEs) and their impact on student learning.
4. Offer a minimum of 5 research-based strategies for creating a trauma-informed classroom, with direct mention of at least 1 research study supporting each strategy.

(Continued)

> **Textbox 5.4 (Continued)**
>
> **5** Offer a minimum of 5 specific practices that will be implemented in your classroom to make it trauma informed, with specific descriptions of how implementation will happen.
>
> **6** Describe the responsibilities of all parties in the classroom (teacher, paraprofessional, students, families/caregivers) in implementing those practices.
>
> **7** Describe how the effectiveness of those practices will be evaluated.
>
> **8** Include a minimum of 7 peer-reviewed references that are mentioned in the video.
>
> When you submit your video, you also need to submit two additional Microsoft Word documents:
>
> **1** A complete transcript of the video. It is likely that your video software can provide a transcript for you, but you will need to check it to fix any errors.
>
> **2** An APA-formatted reference page that lists each of the references mentioned in the video.
>
> If you have any questions about the expectations for this assignment, please reach out to your course instructor as soon as possible. Please pay close attention to each of the guidelines above, as you will be graded on each of these things.

Let's Practice—"We Do"

Dr. Liu is the professor for a secondary teaching methods course. Her students include future teachers in all subject areas, so she aims to create assessments that are appropriate for all of her students. Dr. Liu is planning a unit on using explicit and direct instruction to teach academic content and is trying to design a summative assessment that is appropriate for all subject areas. A few of her students are currently serving as long-term subs in the local school district, so Dr. Liu would like to design an assessment for this unit that her students can immediately use in their own jobs. However, not all of her students are currently working in schools, so she wants to be careful to develop an assessment that will also meet the learning needs of her students who are not yet teaching.

Now it is time to practice. This is the "We Do" part of good teaching. Answer the questions in Textbox 5.5 using the blank spaces provided. Once

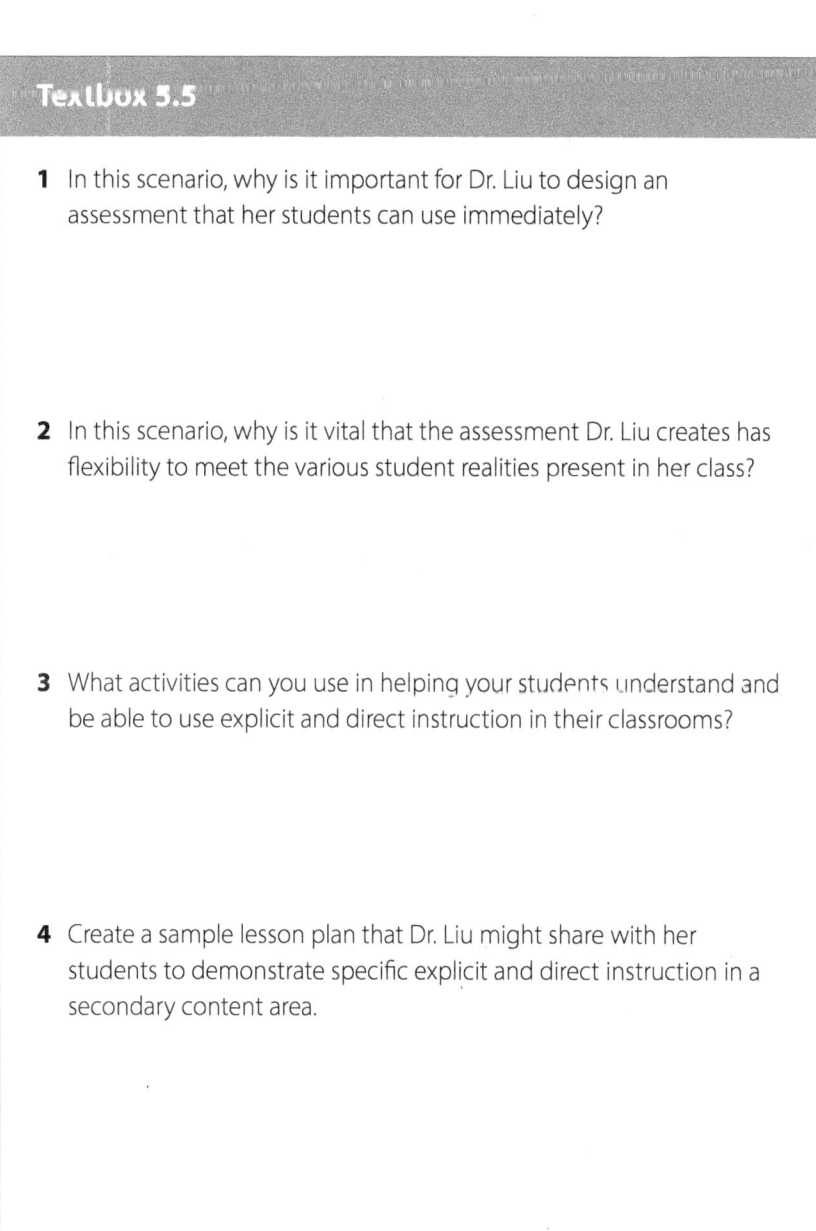

Textbox 5.5

1 In this scenario, why is it important for Dr. Liu to design an assessment that her students can use immediately?

2 In this scenario, why is it vital that the assessment Dr. Liu creates has flexibility to meet the various student realities present in her class?

3 What activities can you use in helping your students understand and be able to use explicit and direct instruction in their classrooms?

4 Create a sample lesson plan that Dr. Liu might share with her students to demonstrate specific explicit and direct instruction in a secondary content area.

you have your answers, share them on social media using the hashtag #OnlineTeacherPrep and tagging us. You may also take a look at the suggestions included in Appendix A if you get stumped (or need a little validation that you know what you are doing).

Apply to Your Own Courses—"You Do"

It is now your time to practice designing high-quality assessments in your own online course. Follow the steps in Textbox 5.6. Once you complete these steps, you will have one idea ready to implement in your next online course. If you feel like sharing with us or others, please share on social media!

> **Textbox 5.6**
>
> **1** Identify a course you teach. List the name of the course here.
>
> **2** Choose one learning objective addressed in that course and the formative or summative assessment you currently use to evaluate student mastery of that learning objective. Now choose a strategy discussed in this chapter that you can use to evaluate the learning objective.

> **Textbox 5.6 (Continued)**
>
> 3 List the original assessment directions step by step in a table. Highlight the parts you can change. In the table, in the next column, write out how you will change the direction. Do this for each highlighted direction.
>
> 4 Remember this assessment, and when you get to Chapter 7, pull it out and you can use your newly updated assessment to recreate your grading rubric.
>
> Please note that we are not asking you to create an entirely new assessment (unless you want to do so). Instead, we are asking you to build on work you have already done to incorporate more high-quality authentic assessment strategies.
>
> **Congratulations!**—You have just started the process of incorporating high-quality assessments into your online class! Now try it again for another course or another week in the same course.

References

Aguilar, J. J., & Flores, Y. (2022). Analyzing the effectiveness of using mixed-reality simulations to develop elementary pre-service teacher's high-leverage practices in a mathematics methods course. *EURASIA Journal of Mathematics, Science and Technology Education, 18*(5). Article em2107.

Ajjawi, R., Tai, J., Dollinger, M., Dawson, P., Boud, D., & Bearman, M. (2024). From authentic assessment to authenticity in assessment: Broadening perspectives. *Assessment & Evaluation in Higher Education, 49*(4), 499–510. https://doi.org/10.1080/02602938.2023.2271193

Allemang, B., Dimitropoulos, G., Collins, T., Gill, P., Fulton, A., McLaughlin, A.-M., Ayala, J., Blaug, C., Judge-Stasiak, A., & Letkemann, L. (2022). Role plays to enhance readiness for practicum: Perceptions of graduate & undergraduate social work students. *Journal of Social Work Education, 58*(4), 652–666. https://doi.org/10.1080/10437797.2021.1957735

Almeida, T., Silva, C., & Rosa, J. (2021). Invented spelling intervention programmes: Comparing explicit and implicit instructions. *Análise Psicológica, 39*(2), 229–245. https://doi.org/10.14417/ap.1848

Altınay, Z. (2016). Evaluating peer learning and assessment in online collaborative learning environments. *Behaviour & Information Technology, 36*(3), 312–320. https://doi.org/10.1080/0144929X.2016.1232752

Ashman, G., Kalyuga, S., & Sweller, J. (2020). Problem-solving or explicit instruction: Which should go first when element interactivity is high? *Educational Psychology Review, 32*(1), 229–247. https://doi.org/10.1007/s10648-019-09500-5

Azim, S., & Khan, M. (2012). Authentic assessment: An instructional tool to enhance students learning. *Academic Research International, 2*(3), 314–320. https://ecommons.aku.edu/pakistan_ied_pdcc/11

Bakir, N., Humpherys, S., & Dana, K. (2020). Students' perceptions of challenges and solutions to face-to-face and online group work. *Information Systems Education Journal, 18*(5), 75–88.

Boothe, K. A., Lohmann, M. J., & Owiny, R. L. (2020). Enhancing student learning in the online instructional environment through the use of Universal Design for Learning. *Networks: An Online Journal for Teacher Research, 22*(1). https://doi.org/10.4148/2470-6353.1310

Budin, S. (2024). Three approaches to using mixed reality simulations for teacher preparation and recruitment of future teachers. *Education Sciences, 14*(1), 75. https://doi.org/10.3390/educsci14010075

Carney, E. A., Zhang, X., Charsha, A., Taylor, J. N., & Hoshaw, J. P. (2022). Formative assessment helps students learn over time: Why aren't we paying more attention to it? *Intersection: A Journal at the Intersection of Assessment and Learning, 4*(1).

Darling-Hammond, L., Herman, J., Pellegrino, J., Abedi, J., Aber, J. L., Baker, E., Bennett, R., Gordon, E., Haertel, E., Hakuta, K., Ho, A., Linn, R. L., Pearson, P. D., Popham, J., Resnick, L., Schoenfeld, A. H., Shavelson, R., Shepard, L. A., Shulman, L., & Steele, C. M. (2013). *Criteria for high-quality assessment*. Stanford Center for Opportunity Policy in Education.

Driver, M. K., Zimmer, K. E., Khan, O., Sadler, J. V., & Draper, E. (2024). Preparing general education teachers for inclusive settings: Integrating high-leverage practices and mixed-reality simulation in pre-service coursework. *Education Sciences, 14*(4), 428. https://doi.org/10.3390/educsci14040428

Ellis, C., van Haeringen, K., Harper, R., Bretag, T., Zucker, I., McBride, S., Rozenberg, P., Newton, P., & Saddiqui, S. (2020). Does authentic assessment assure academic integrity? Evidence from contract cheating data. *Higher Education Research & Development, 39*(3), 454–469. https://doi.org/10.1080/07294360.2019.1680956

Flaherty, H. B. (2023). Teaching note—Using technology to enhance experiential learning through simulated role plays. *Journal of Social Work Education, 59*(4), 1294–1300. https://doi.org./10.1080/10437797.2022.2050869

Gallagher, T. L., García, P. O., Vokatis, B., Johnson, T., & Cavendish, L. (2024). Preparing tutors for assessment, data-based instruction, and reflective practice. *Literacy Practice & Research, 49*(1), 1 23.

Hilliard, J., Kear, K., Donelan, H., & Heaney, C. (2020). Students' experiences of anxiety in an assessed, online collaborative project. *Computers & Education, 143*, Article 103675. https://doi.org/10.1016/j.compedu.2019.103675

Ibarra-Sáiz, M. S., Rodríguez-Gómez, G., & Boud, D. (2021). The quality of assessment tasks as a determinant of learning. *Assessment & Evaluation in Higher Education, 46*(6), 943–955. https://doi.org.ezproxy.ccu.edu/10.1080/02602938.2020.1828268

Kibble, J. D. (2017). Best practices in summative assessment. *Advances in Physiology Education, 41*(1), 110–119. https://journals.physiology.org/doi/full/10.1152/advan.00116.2016

Krzykowski, L., & Kinser, K. (2014). Transparency in student learning assessment: Can accreditation standards make a difference? *Change: The Magazine of Higher Learning, 46*(3), 67–73. https://doi.org/10.1080/00091383.2014.905428

Lohmann, M. J. (2023). *The teacher's guide to action research for special education in PK–12 classrooms.* Rowman & Littlefield.

Manis, A. A., McKenna, L. W., & Schulthorp, S. (2022). Systematic assessment of learning in higher education: A comprehensive approach within curriculum design. *Educational Research Quarterly, 46*(1), 33–45.

Mathers, C. E., Finney, S. J., & Hathcoat, J. D. (2018). Student learning in higher education: A longitudinal analysis and faculty discussion. *Assessment & Evaluation in Higher Education, 43*(8), 1211–1227. https://doi.org/10.1080/02602938.2018.1443202

McClendon, K., & Ho, T. (2016). Building a quality assessment process for measuring and documenting student learning. *Assessment Update, 28*(2), 7–14.

McConnell, D. (2002). The experience of collaborative assessment in e-learning. *Studies in Continuing Education, 24*(1), 73–92. https://doi.org/10.1080/01580370220130459

Murdoch, A., Morrison, J. Q., & Strickler, W. (2024). Process evaluation of a problem-solving approach for analyzing literacy practice within a multi-tiered system of supports framework. *Behavior & Social Issues, 33*(1), 479–503. https://doi.org/10.1007/s42822-024-00166-5

Nel, C., & Marais, E. (2023). Pre-service teachers' perceptions on eliciting learners' knowledge in a mixed-reality simulation environment. *Reading & Writing: Journal of the Literacy Association of South Africa, 14*(1).

Ng, R., O'Reilly, C. L., Collins, J. C., Roennfeldt, H., McMillan, S. S., Wheeler, A. J., & El-Den, S. (2023). Mental Health First Aid crisis role-plays between pharmacists and simulated patients with lived experience: A thematic analysis of debrief. *Social Psychiatry & Psychiatric Epidemiology, 58*(9), 1365–1373. https://doi.org/10.1007/s00127-023-02443-x

Romero, G. C., & González, F. M. (2023). Assessment for learning: Tensions and challenges in the framework of learning outcomes energized through teaching practice—Case of Universidad de la Costa–UNICOSTA. *Procedia Computer Science, 224*, 519–524. https://doi.org.ezproxy.ccu.edu/10.1016/j.procs.2023.09.075

Scherling, S. E. (2011). Designing and fostering effective online group projects. *Adult Learning, 22*(2), 13–18. https://doi.org/10.1177/104515951102200202

Shepard, L. A. (2000). The role of assessment in a learning culture. *Educational Researcher, 29*(7), 4–14.

Weng, C., Puspitasari, D., Rathinasabapathi, A., & Kuo, A. (2022). Reflective learning as an important key to the success of an online course. *Behaviour & Information Technology, 41*(15), 3382–3398. https://doi.org/10.1080/0144929X.2021.1988145

Wiggins, G. (1990). The case for authentic assessment. *Practical Assessment, Research, and Evaluation, 2*(1), Article 2. https://doi.org/10.7275/ffb1-mm19

6 Assessing Student Learning

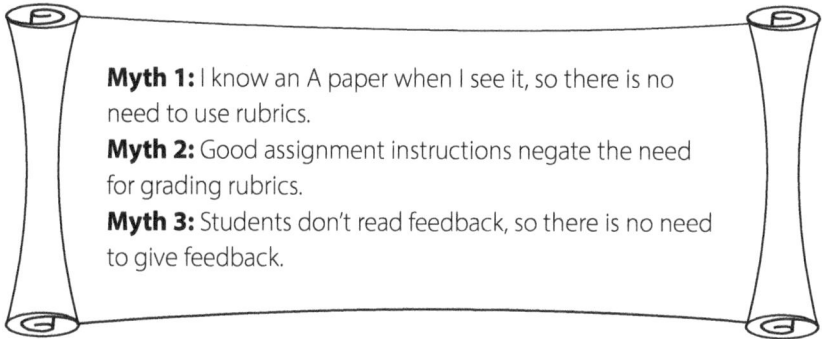

Myth 1: I know an A paper when I see it, so there is no need to use rubrics.
Myth 2: Good assignment instructions negate the need for grading rubrics.
Myth 3: Students don't read feedback, so there is no need to give feedback.

Debunking the Myths

In the last chapter, we talked about designing assessments that are authentic and accurately assess student mastery of course learning objectives. This short chapter expands on that discussion by sharing information about assessment tools we recommend using in your online classroom. Please don't get the impression that this, being the shortest chapter in the book, is an indication of the importance of this topic—it is not! Before we get into our suggested assessment tools, we want to tackle a few myths.

The first myth is the idea that good university instructors, especially those with significant experience in both PK–12 and higher education classrooms, can easily recognize high-quality work versus student assignments that do not meet expectations. Marla once spoke to another professor who said, "I know an A paper when I see it, so there is no need for grading criteria or a rubric in my courses." While we do understand this sentiment, the reality is that all teachers, including teacher educators, do have some bias when grading. The literature indicates that teachers may demonstrate bias in grading based on factors unrelated to the assignment or the course learning objectives (Malouff & Thorsteinsson, 2016). Factors that may impact grades include, but are not limited to, (a) student race (Chin et al., 2020; Quinn, 2020), (b) student gender (Copur-Gencturk et al., 2020; Doornkamp et al., 2022), (c) student behaviors (Contreras, 2023; Ferman & Fontes, 2022), and (d) teacher emotions while grading (Brackett et al., 2013).

Grading can be a subjective activity, and there is inherent bias in the process, which will impact the way teacher educators grade assignments. We likely can spot a high-quality paper and easily identify papers (and other assignment submissions) that do not meet expectations. But we may not be completely accurate and equitable in grading student work without good assessment tools. Two students may submit identical work to two different course instructors (or even the same instructor), but one student receives a B and the other receives a C+. The use of assessment tools helps to ensure that student work is graded equitably and fairly by all faculty, removing bias (to the extent possible) from the evaluations of student learning. The key to this is to create the assessment tools with others and to ensure interrater reliability.

A second myth we hear is that we don't need to use rubrics if we spend sufficient time developing high-quality assignments that outline exactly what we want students to do. Again, we understand this thinking, but it is somewhat flawed. As noted in Chapter 5, good assignment instructions are vital for student success. But those must be paired with explicit information on how the work will be assessed. Assignment instructions tell students what is expected in the assignment. The rubric tells the students how those specific expectations will be evaluated (Panadero & Jonsson, 2013).

Consider this scenario: pretend you are a student who has been told you will need to include four peer-reviewed citations, six direct applications to your classroom, and no APA or grammatical errors in the submission. However, as an online learner with a full-time job and a family, you have many competing priorities and know that you won't have time to complete all assignment requirements before the work is due, so you must make decisions about how to best utilize your time. The assignment instructions gave you guidance on what to do but did not tell you which of those three requirements will be graded most heavily. Knowing that 60% of the assignment grade will be based on the applications in your classroom and the other two requirements are each worth 20% of the grade would help you decide to focus more of your time on application of learning. We know that, as teachers, we want our students to give 100% to all parts of their work. But this is simply not always realistic for them (and it is not always realistic for us in our jobs). Sometimes we do have to make hard decisions about how to best focus our time—rubrics help students make informed decisions.

The final myth we hear is that students don't read the grading feedback that faculty provide, so taking time to offer feedback is not worth the effort. We completely understand this sentiment. The reality is that some students don't read the feedback. And in some courses, our learning management system (LMS) analytics may tell us that very few students read it. But Cunningham (2019) found that higher-achieving students do read assignment feedback and use that feedback to support them in future assignment tasks. Providing high-quality feedback is good practice and does support the learning of some students, which makes it worth our time and effort, despite any challenges in providing that feedback.

Tools to Use—"I Do"

A variety of tools are available for supporting student success with course assessments. Below, we offer our top four recommended tools: (a) rubrics, (b) exemplars, (c) specific feedback, and (d) varied feedback tools.

1 Rubrics

Our first recommendation is to provide students with the grading rubric when assigning all coursework, including formative assessments, summative assessments, and asynchronous discussions. A rubric is a tool that outlines what is expected in the assignment and how each expected component will be graded; rubrics should include task descriptions, scales, and dimensions with descriptors (Stevens & Levi, 2023). Students appreciate when faculty provide grading rubrics when assigning coursework and report that the use of rubrics helps clarify expectations for assignments (Jonsson, 2014), leading to more students meeting the assignment expectations (Krebs et al., 2022). The use of rubrics may also reduce student anxiety regarding expectations and grading, especially for English language learners (Arindra & Ardi, 2020).

In our experience, writing high-quality rubrics aligned to the specific assignment can be very time consuming, but the time spent on the work is worth it for student success. Some university faculty lean toward using the single-point rubric (Chao et al., 2021), while others create rubrics that are more expansive with several columns (Allen & Tanner, 2006). And some faculty even include students in the development of rubrics (Morton et al., 2021).

Over the years, we have both tried a variety of rubric formats; for the most part, we have found that the quality of guidance included in the rubric has a larger impact on student learning than does the specific rubric format. Figure 6.1 offers an example of a rubric Marla might create for one of her course assignments in which students are asked to read an article and share, in a manner of their choosing, what they learned and how it applies to their own classroom instruction. Marla always includes an "Exceeds Expectations" column in her rubrics. In order for students to be scored in this column, they

	Exceeds expectations	**Meets expectations**	**Does not meet expectations**
Selected article 25% of grade	25 points The selected article is available from the university library, is peer reviewed, is less than 5 years old, and is not a course material. The APA citation for the article has no errors.	23–24 points The selected article is available from the university library, is peer reviewed, and is not a course material. It may be more than 5 years old but less than 10 years old, or there may be one error in the APA citation for the article.	0–22 points The selected article is not available from the university library Or Is not peer reviewed Or Is more than 10 years old Or Is a course material Or There are 2+ errors in the APA citation.
Takeaways 25% of grade	25 points The submission includes at least 10 takeaways/key points from the article.	23–24 points The submission includes at least 8 takeaways/key points from the article.	0–22 points The submission includes fewer than 8 takeaways/key points from the article.

Figure 6.1 Sample Rubric. *(Continued)*

	Exceeds expectations	**Meets expectations**	**Does not meet expectations**
Personal application 25% of grade	25 points The submission includes a list of at least 5 personal applications, describing how the teacher candidate plans to use what he/she learned from the article in his/her own classroom. Descriptions offer specific information, including an action plan for implementation.	23–24 points The submission includes a list of at least 3 personal applications, describing how the teacher candidate plans to use what he/she learned from the article in his/her own classroom. Descriptions offer specific information, including an action plan for implementation.	0–22 points The submission includes fewer than 3 personal applications Or The applications do not include action plans Or The applications are not appropriate for the teacher candidate's teaching position Or The applications described do not align with the article selected.
Burning questions 25% of grade	25 points The submission includes at least 5 questions the student has about the article topic.	23–24 points The submission includes at least 3 questions the student has about the article topic.	0–22 points The submission includes fewer than 3 questions Or The questions are not related to the article topic.

Figure 6.1 Sample Rubric.

must do more than is required—doing so is the only way to get 100% on assessments in her courses. When students meet the requirements for the assessment, they are scored in the "meets expectations" category and will get an A on the assignment, but not full credit. Students who do not meet all expectations will receive a B or lower on the assessment. Kathy has found that when using the "exceeds expectations" column for her rubrics, she had to talk to the students about what that means grade-wise, as Marla mentioned above. This is because many students do not feel they should have to do "more" than the required to get an A.

2 Exemplars

We know that this second recommendation will likely be a bit controversial. But we also know that students often need examples of high-quality work. Bacchus et al. (2019) found that students are more likely to meet assignment expectations when university faculty provide both a rubric and an exemplar; together, these tools help reduce confusion and increase clarity regarding expectations. Additionally, the use of examples can support students in self-monitoring while completing their work as they can compare their own work to the provided example (Hawe et al., 2020). With all of that in mind, we suggest offering exemplars for completed assignments when appropriate. To do this, you may choose to create your own example or you may use an assignment submitted by a student in a previous semester, being sure to get permission from that student and removing all identifying information from the sample.

When she first started teaching online and was overwhelmed by the workload, Marla used lesson plans written by program graduates as examples for her teacher candidates in their field courses. She selected a few examples that showed students both A+ work and work that met expectations but did not necessarily exceed expectations. Over time, she has replaced the work of students with lesson plans she has written. Especially for her special education alternative licensure candidates, this practice of sharing high-quality lesson plans that are aligned with state standards, tailored to PK–12 student needs and individualized education program (IEP) goals, and meet all program expectations has led to improved lesson plan writing by Marla's students.

3 Specific Feedback

In the myths, we discussed the fact that feedback is critical for student learning. Now we want to expand on that statement a bit. Feedback is critical, but it must be specific and timely (Percell, 2017). Dawson et al. (2018) report that students seek feedback that is specific to their assignment submissions and offers guidance on ways to improve their work. The use of feedback helps students understand why they earned a certain grade on an assessment and supports their further learning.

We spend hours offering feedback to our students, through both general feedback to the entire class and specific feedback to students. Recently,

Marla taught a course in which about half of the students did not use APA formatting for a research paper they submitted. Her university requires APA in all graduate courses, so Marla assumed the students were familiar with the expectations. When she realized that many were not, she posted a course announcement (see Chapter 1) that included a reminder that APA is required, a short video she created about APA, an APA template, and links to web-based resources with information about APA 7th edition guidelines. In other courses, only one or two students do not follow APA guidelines, so she offers this guidance in individual grading feedback to those students.

When we offer grading feedback, we focus on being as specific as possible and offering students both guidance on improvements and rhetorical questions to further their thinking about the topic of the assessment. We try to ensure that our feedback includes both areas of strength and suggestions for improvement. Common feedback statements we use include:

- "I appreciate that you mentioned you plan to implement this teaching strategy in your classroom. Can you tell me more? What might this look like in your classroom? What action steps will you take to implement this strategy?"
- "Be sure that you are using APA formatting for all references. Only the first word of the article title should be capitalized, and the journal name should be in italics."
- "Thank you for identifying resources to support the statements you made in this paper. Remember that not all resources are credible and you need to use caution when citing blogs and .com websites. The information you cited from Miss Peggy's Kinder Kids blog regarding learning styles is not accurate and does not align with what we know about this theory from research."

4 Varied Feedback Tools

As we noted above, feedback is important. And we know that many online faculty default to using text-based feedback for all grading. While this can be convenient, it is not the only option. Just like students can submit work in a variety of mediums, we can assess their work using various tools. Varied feedback can be achieved through many LMS tools, including tools where you can write your feedback to students, either through a rubric or as a stand-alone. You are also able to annotate on student papers through many LMSs. You may choose to meet with your students one-on-one to provide feedback. Yet another way may be to provide audio or video snippets attached to individual assignments.

When students are provided with audio feedback, their likelihood of engaging with the feedback increases as compared to engagement with text-based feedback (Lunt & Curran, 2009). Students report that audio feedback feels more personal because they are able to hear the instructor's voice (Voelkel & Mello, 2014). Similar results were found for video-based feedback. Some students prefer the personal nature of this format in comparison to written feedback (West & Turner, 2015). It should be noted, though, that there is no strong evidence to support whether audio- or video-based feedback improves student course outcomes (Mahoney et al., 2018).

For many students, the use of varied feedback formats also increases student course satisfaction (Sarcona et al., 2020). It should be noted, though, that some studies have found that students prefer more traditional text-based feedback (Lowenthal, 2021). Because it does appear that student preferences differ and there is no strong evidence about outcomes, we recommend that faculty utilize a variety of formats for offering feedback within their course.

Kathy has a colleague who uses video-based feedback when he grades major assignments. He uses Yuja (integrated into the LMS) to record himself grading. He first previews the student work and then starts the video recording. He screen-shares the assignment and highlights specific parts of the submission as he talks to the student about their work. He offers guidance on positives about the submission, as well as areas for improvement. Once the video is complete, he posts a link to the recording in the grading section for the specific assignment in the LMS. Based on the specific assignment and the feedback necessary to support students, these videos may range in length from two minutes to fifteen minutes. Students have reported that they appreciate this video-based feedback method.

Avoid This

As we have done in previous chapters, we also want to share with you some teaching practices that you should avoid when grading student assessments.

1 Too much time spent on feedback

Giving high-quality feedback is important, but the reality is that providing feedback can be very time consuming. You could work full time just grading and giving feedback for one course. But that is not a productive use of your time. There is certainly a point where more is not better, and we do not recommend spending too much time giving feedback. We cannot tell you exactly how to do this, as the answer will be different based on your teaching style and the specific needs of your students and course content, but we do have a few recommendations for reducing the time it takes to give high-quality feedback. First, we suggest creating a feedback bank. This is just a Word document in which you have common feedback statements that you might need or want to use. Instead of typing the same statement each time, you can simply copy and paste from the feedback bank. This can be an especially useful strategy for feedback on APA or grammar, as well as for common misconceptions about the assignment content. Another strategy is to set a timer for each assignment. Only give yourself as long as the timer allows to grade and provide feedback. When the timer goes off, you should fill out the rubric and post the assignment grade. With this strategy, though, we do suggest allowing yourself one or two (or more for a larger class) student submissions that get double grading time because more extensive feedback is needed to support that specific student. Finally, you can reduce the time spent offering feedback by using the strategy noted above about classwide feedback when appropriate.

2 Not aligning grading with the rubric

The second practice we recommend avoiding is not using the rubric exactly as written. We have seen some faculty who use the rubric as a starting point, but then adjust student points based on various factors. Most of the times that we have seen this, the instructor is trying to help the student get a better grade and is showing empathy to struggling learners. But we would argue that this practice does not really help the student in the long run. If students learn that rubrics are more suggestions for grading rather than grading guidelines, they will quickly learn not to follow the rubric. In addition, when students are not meeting expectations, they need to be aware of this and be graded accordingly. We believe a more empathetic approach, and one that will better support student learning, is to grade per the rubric, provide high-quality feedback, and allow the student the opportunity to redo the assignment.

3 Having one rubric for all assessments

The final practice we recommend avoiding is using the exact same rubric for all assessments. We have seen some faculty who have one discussion rubric, one written paper rubric, and one presentation rubric—they use these three rubrics for all assignments in their courses. Rubrics should be tailored to the unique learning goals and requirements for the specific assignment. When rubrics are designed to address the specific assignment, students are provided with better guidance on what is expected. With that being said, we also do not recommend starting from square one every time you write a rubric. You can have a few basic rubrics that you use as starting points and then adapt the appropriate rubric when you create an assignment.

Let's Practice—"We Do"

In Chapter 5, we met Dr. Liu, who was teaching students about explicit and direct instruction. She has designed her assessment, and now she needs to create a rubric and a feedback plan. One of her colleagues has told her that it is important to do this step before giving the assessment to students. But she is a bit unsure where to start.

Now it is time to practice. This is the "We Do" part of good teaching. Answer the questions in Textbox 6.1 using the blank spaces provided. Once you have your answers, share them on social media using the hashtag #OnlineTeacherPrep and tagging both of us in your post. You may also take a look at the suggestions included in Appendix A if you get stumped (or need a little validation that you know what you are doing).

Textbox 6.1

1 Describe to Dr. Liu why she needs to provide students with the rubric when giving them the assessment.

2 Based on the assessment that you designed in Chapter 5, create a rubric that Dr. Liu might use to evaluate student submissions.

3 Considering both the assessment topic and the rubric you created, consider the type of feedback that Dr. Liu should use when grading this assessment. What might be the benefits and drawbacks of written, audio, and video feedback?

Apply to Your Own Courses—"You Do"

It is now your time to practice designing authentic assessments in your own online course. Follow the steps in Textbox 6.2. Once you complete these steps, you will have one idea ready to implement in your next online course.

> **Textbox 6.2**
>
> **1** In Chapter 5, you designed an assessment that you can use in your own classroom. Create a rubric for that assessment.
>
> **2** Make a plan for how you will provide feedback when grading that assessment.
>
> **3** In Chapter 3, you created an asynchronous discussion for one of your courses. Create a rubric for that discussion.
>
> **Congratulations!**—You now have a well developed rubric to use in your online class. Now, try creating a rubric for another new activity you have recently created.

References

Ajjawi, R., Tai, J., Dollinger, M., Dawson, P., Boud, D., & Bearman, M. (2024). From authentic assessment to authenticity in assessment: Broadening perspectives. *Assessment & Evaluation in Higher Education, 49*(4), 499–510. https://doi.org/10.1080/02602938.2023.2271193

Allen, D., & Tanner, K. (2006). Rubrics: Tools for making learning goals and evaluation criteria explicit for both teachers and learners. *Life Sciences Education, 5*(3), 197–295. https://doi.org/10.1187/cbe.06-06-0168

Arindra, M. Y., & Ardi, P. (2020). The correlation between students' writing anxiety and the use of writing assessment rubrics. *LEARN Journal: Language Education and Acquisition Research Network, 13*(1), 76–93.

Bacchus, R., Colvin, E., Knight, E. B., & Ritter, L. (2019). When rubrics aren't enough: Exploring exemplars and student rubric co-construction. *Journal of Curriculum and Pedagogy, 17*(1), 48–61. https://doi.org/10.1080/15505170.2019.1627617

Brackett, M. A., Floman, J. L., Ashton-James, C., Cherkasskiy, L., & Salovey, P. (2013). The influence of teacher emotion on grading practices: A preliminary look at the evaluation of student writing. *Teachers and Teaching, 19*(6), 634–646. https://doi.org/10.1080/13540602.2013.827453

Chao, I. C. I., King, S., Gotch, C. M., & Roduta Roberts, M. (2021). Exploring the educational impact of using a single-point rubric through validation in interprofessional education. *Journal of Allied Health, 50*(4), 253–266.

Chin, M. J., Quinn, D. M., Dhaliwal, T. K., & Lovison, V. S. (2020). Bias in the air: A nationwide exploration of teachers' implicit racial attitudes, aggregate bias, and student outcomes. *Educational Researcher, 49*(8), 566–578. https://doi.org/10.3102/0013189X20937240

Contreras, D. (2023). Gender differences in grading: Teacher bias or student behaviour? *Education Economics, 32*(6), 762–785. https://doi.org/10.1080/09645292.2023.2252620

Copur-Gencturk, Y., Cimpian, J. R., Lubienski, S. T., & Thacker, I. (2020). Teachers' bias against the mathematical ability of female, black, and Hispanic students. *Educational Researcher, 49*(1), 30–43. https://doi.org/10.3102/0013189X19890577

Cunningham, J. M. (2019). Composition students' opinions of and attention to instructor feedback. *Journal of Response to Writing, 5*(1), Article 3. https://scholarsarchive.byu.edu/journalrw/vol5/iss1/3

Dawson, P., Henderson, M., Mahoney, P., Phillips, M., Ryan, T., Boud, D., & Molloy, E. (2018). What makes for effective feedback: Staff and student perspectives. *Assessment & Evaluation in Higher Education, 44*(1), 25–36. https://doi.org/10.1080/02602938.2018.1467877

Doornkamp, L., van der Pol, L. D., Groeneveld, S., Mesman, J., Endendijk, J. J., & Groeneveld, M. G. (2022). Understanding gender bias in teachers' grading: The role of gender stereotypical beliefs. *Teaching and Teacher Education, 118*, 103826. https://doi.org/10.1016/j.tate.2022.103826

Ellis, C., van Haeringen, K., Harper, R., Bretag, T., Zucker, I., McBride, S., Rozenberg, P., Newton, P., & Saddiqui, S. (2020). Does authentic assessment assure academic integrity? Evidence from contract cheating data. *Higher Education Research & Development, 39*(3), 454–469. https://doi.org/10.1080/07294360.2019.1680956

Ferman, B., & Fontes, L. F. (2022). Assessing knowledge or classroom behavior: Evidence of teachers' grading bias. *Journal of Public Economics, 216*. https://doi.org/10.1016/j.jpubeco.2022.104773

Hawe, E., Dixon, H., Murray, J., & Chandler, S. (2020). Using rubrics and exemplars to develop students' evaluative and productive knowledge and skill. *Journal of Further and Higher Education, 45*(8), 1033–1047. https://doi.org/10.1080/0309877X.2020.1851358

Jonsson, A. (2014). Rubrics as a way of providing transparency in assessment. *Assessment & Evaluation in Higher Education, 39*(7), 840–852. https://doi.org/10.1080/02602938.2013.875117

Krebs, R., Rothstein, B., & Roelle, J. (2022). Rubrics enhance accuracy and reduce cognitive load in self-assessment. *Metacognition Learning, 17*, 627–650. https://doi.org/10.1007/s11409-022-09302-1

Lowenthal, P. R. (2021). Video feedback: Is it worth the effort? A response to Borup et al. *Education Technology Research and Development, 69*, 127–131. https://doi.org/10.1007/s11423-020-09872-4

Lunt, T., & Curran, J. (2009). "Are you listening please?" The advantages of electronic audio feedback compared to written feedback. *Assessment & Evaluation in Higher Education, 35*(7), 759–769. https://doi.org/10.1080/02602930902977772

Mahoney, P., Macfarlane, S., & Ajjawi, R. (2018). A qualitative synthesis of video feedback in higher education. *Teaching in Higher Education, 24*(2), 157–179. https://doi.org/10.1080/13562517.2018.1471457

Malouff, J. M., & Thorsteinsson, E. B. (2016). Bias in grading: A meta-analysis of experimental research findings. *Australian Journal of Education, 60*(3), 245–256. https://doi.org/10.1177/0004944116664618

Morton, J. K., Northcote, M., Kilgour, P., & Jackson, W. A. (2021). Sharing the construction of assessment rubrics with students: A model for collaborative rubric construction. *Journal of University Teaching & Learning Practice, 18*(4), 98–111. https://doi.org/10.53761/1.18.4.9

Panadero, E., & Jonsson, A. (2013). The use of scoring rubrics for formative assessment purposes revisited: A review. *Educational Research Review, 9*, 129–144. https://doi.org/10.1016/j.edurev.2013.01.002

Percell, J. C. (2017). Lessons from alternative grading: Essential qualities of teacher feedback. *The Clearing House: A Journal of Educational Strategies, Issues and Ideas, 90*(4), 111–115. https://doi.org/10.1080/00098655.2017.1304067

Quinn, D. M. (2020). Experimental evidence on teachers' racial bias in student evaluation: The role of grading scales. *Educational Evaluation and Policy Analysis, 42*(3), 375–392. https://doi.org/10.3102/0162373720932188

Sarcona, A., Dirhan, D., & Davidson, P. (2020). An overview of audio and written feedback from students' and instructors' perspective. *Educational Media International, 57*(1), 47–60. https://doi.org/10.1080/09523987.2020.1744853

Stevens, D. D., & Levi, A. J. (2023). *Introduction to rubrics: An assessment tool to save grading time, convey effective feedback, and promote student learning* (2nd ed.). Routledge. https://doi.org/10.4324/9781003445432

Voelkel, S., & Mello, L. V. (2014). Audio feedback—Better feedback? *Bioscience Education, 22*(1), 16–30. https://doi.org/10.11120/beej.2014.00022

West, J., & Turner, W. (2015). Enhancing the assessment experience: Improving student perceptions, engagement and understanding using online video feedback. *Innovations in Education and Teaching International, 53*(4), 400–410. https://doi.org/10.1080/14703297.2014.1003954

7 The Reflective Practitioner

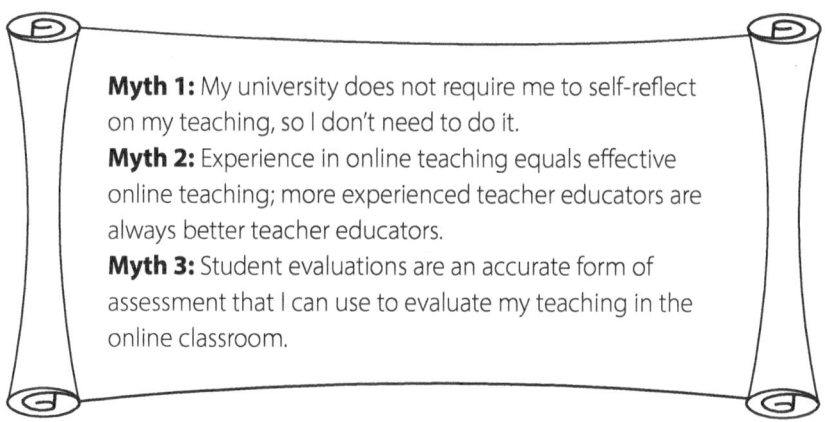

Myth 1: My university does not require me to self-reflect on my teaching, so I don't need to do it.
Myth 2: Experience in online teaching equals effective online teaching; more experienced teacher educators are always better teacher educators.
Myth 3: Student evaluations are an accurate form of assessment that I can use to evaluate my teaching in the online classroom.

Debunking the Myths

You are done creating your courses and developing (or re-developing) assignments and activities. At this point, you have a good grasp on your grading and feedback, so you are now a perfect online instructor, right? Wrong! There is still more to do to be good teachers, model good instructional practices, and grow your own skills. We must be reflective on our teaching journey and continue to do so for our entire careers. The reality is that none of us will ever stop learning and growing as teachers—there is always more to know than we can ever possibly learn. This chapter will debunk the myths regarding being a reflective teacher educator, as well as provide you with some tools that we have used to help us reflect on our own teaching and improve our professional skills.

The first myth we want to address is that self-reflection is not required, thus making it an unnecessary use of your time. Whether or not something is required is not enough reason *not* to do something. We are all educators who are educating those who will, or are, in the trenches of PK–12 schools. We must practice what we preach and model good teaching practices to our own students. We expect our students to reflect on their teaching and the learning of their students; we need to do the same. We know you have countless demands on your time. The reality is that being a professor is hard, and there are never enough hours in the day to complete all the tasks on our to-do lists. Trust us when we say that we feel the same way. Sometimes, taking the time to reflect on our teaching feels more like a "nice to do" rather than a "need to do" task in comparison to university obligations, service commitments, teaching courses, responding to emails, attending meetings, presenting at conferences, and research and publishing work (phew—we really do a lot!). However, we know that good teaching matters for our students and, ultimately, their students, even if it is not as highly valued by the university as other tasks.

In Chapter 5, we talked about remote field experience observations. One tool we shared in that chapter is the use of student reflection. Just as it is important for our students to reflect on their teaching, it is also vital for teacher educators to do so. According to Wlodarsky (2005), university faculty who engage in reflective practices regarding their own instruction are more aware of their own strengths and areas for improvement in the classroom. Hodges and Fowler (2020) note that faculty who engage in quality self-reflection are better able to adapt to the changing needs of students. Basically, what we know is that if we want to be effective online instructors, we have to be reflective about our own teaching strengths and areas of weakness. Self-reflection is necessary for professional growth to occur.

The second myth we need to discuss is that having online teaching experience is the same as quality effective instruction. While experience can improve our skills, it can also cause some people to become increasingly stuck in bad habits and ineffective instructional methodologies. We have all met longtime faculty who are just going through the motions of teaching. This happens with both face-to-face and online faculty. None of us want to be that "dinosaur" that our colleagues all talk about behind our backs. We must stay current in the field and teach in ways that meet the needs of our students, which means we always need to be learning and evaluating our own instruction.

Podolsky et al. (2019) found that more experienced teachers are often more effective in the classroom as measured by student achievement. But, as noted by Kini and Podolsky (2016), this is not always the case, and very experienced teachers can be ineffective. In fact, some research (e.g., Irvine, 2022) indicates that the relationship between teacher experience and teacher effectiveness is complicated and involves several nuances. So, while experience is often correlated with effectiveness in the classroom, there is no guarantee that more experienced teacher educators are more effective than their less-experienced colleagues. On a related note, it is also possible that more effective instructors are more likely to stay in the field longer, which could impact this data. Less effective teaching faculty may choose to move to more research-focused positions or other administrative roles that require less teaching (and, to be clear, we believe that these positions are just as valuable as teaching-focused roles, so this is not a "dig" at others).

The reality is that experienced teachers became effective at their job by continuing to grow professionally and improve their skills. In order to do this, they must take the time to self-reflect on their teaching. While slightly off topic, we want to take this opportunity to remind our readers that, as teacher educators, we need to stay connected with PK–12 schools and spend time in those schools. Especially when teaching online and conducting remote observations, it can be very easy to never actually enter a PK–12 school—the temptation to do all of our work from our home office can be very strong! But this leads to knowledge gaps, which impact our abilities to successfully support our own students in their endeavors to be effective PK–12 teachers. Both Kathy and Marla have worked with very experienced teacher educators who have not entered a school since before the COVID-19 pandemic. While they are good teacher educators who know the research and data about today's schools, their lack of firsthand knowledge about current classroom realities puts their university students at a disadvantage.

Finally, we have to remember that student evaluations are not, in and of themselves, an accurate form of assessment. By now, you have probably been teaching in higher education for a while and have experienced that student evaluations often do not give a clear picture of student learning or teacher effectiveness. This reality that most of us have experienced is supported in the literature. There is bias in how students evaluate faculty based on a variety of factors, including (a) student gender (Heffernan, 2022), (b) faculty gender (Heffernan, 2023), (c) faculty race (Smith & Hawkins, 2011), (d) course subject area (Felkey & Batz-Barbarich, 2021), (e) student age (Tucker, 2014), and (f) student nationality (Tucker, 2014). Students may use these evaluations as a way to share frustrations about their course grades or requirements instead of offering feedback for course improvement (Dana et al., 2023). In fact, there is a direct correlation between student grades in a course and student evaluations in that course, leaving some researchers to suspect that the use of these evaluation tools leads to grade inflation in many cases, especially at universities where student evaluations are a critical component of promotion decisions (Ellis et al., 2003; Stroebe, 2016).

Student evaluations of our teaching are often not accurate reflections of our teaching. Recently, Marla received a very low student evaluation with a comment stating that the student did not think it was fair that Marla uses a rubric to grade all assignments. It is important to note that, as we suggest in Chapter 6, the rubrics are provided to students with the assignment prompts, and Marla tells the students that she will use the rubrics for grading. This specific student rating of Marla's teaching in that course, including the comment about the use of rubrics, negatively impacted her overall teaching evaluation score, but it did not necessarily accurately reflect her teaching effectiveness in the course nor identify areas for teaching improvement.

On the other hand, student evaluations, especially student comments, can offer valuable information that teacher educators can use to evaluate the course. Kathy received a student evaluation last year in which a student described the benefits she received from completing the positive behavior interventions and supports (PBIS) project. The student explained that completing the project helped her to develop an evidence-based classroom management system for her own classroom and that she could already see how doing so benefited her own PK–12 students. The comment also noted that the student wished there were more check-ins with Kathy during the completion of the project to ensure students were on the right track. Based on this student evaluation comment, Kathy has continued including the PBIS project in the course, but she has added two additional checkpoints during the project timeline.

Tools to Use—"I Do"

Above we discuss several myths related to reflection as an instructor. We hope that after reading our explanations of those myths, you will see how reflection can be effective and is an important part of the job, just as it is for those who teach face-to-face—the difference is we need to be a bit more intentional with it. Below you will find some ways of incorporating reflection into our online teaching. If you have other ideas not mentioned, we would love for you to share on social media using the hashtag #OnlineTeacherPrep.

1 Peer Observations

Peer observations in our online classrooms, sometimes referred to as peer review, are a self-reflection strategy we highly recommend. Many universities use peer reviews of teaching as a component of the promotion and tenure process. This is a valuable use of this strategy, but we believe university faculty should engage in peer reviews of teaching at other times in their career as a form of self-reflection for professional growth.

Faculty peer reviews of teaching can be conducted in a variety of ways in the online classroom. One possibility is that the peer reviewer is given access to the course shell for an existing or completed course and spends time looking at discussions, grading, announcements, recorded lectures, and other evidence of teaching. A second option is having the faculty peer reviewer attend a synchronous class session (or multiple class sessions) for a current course. Both strategies have benefits and drawbacks. With either approach, we recommend having a structured checklist, either provided by the university or self-created, that guides what you are looking for in the review. Textbox 7.1 offers a sample review form. Note that the areas for praise outweigh the suggestions for improvement—we do recommend ensuring that you follow this model.

At Marla's university, the first strategy (full access to an entire completed course) is used. When she conducts peer reviews, she enjoys looking at all aspects of the course and getting a good feel for who the faculty member is as a professor. She believes that she learns a lot about her colleagues' instructional practices by doing this. When she is being peer reviewed, however, Marla does get nervous that she might have made a mistake or

Textbox 7.1

Sample Completed Peer Review Form

Name of Faculty Member: Dr. Marla J. Lohmann

Name of Peer Reviewer: Dr. Kathleen A. Boothe

Semester: Fall 2024

Course: Assistive Technology

Areas for Praise

- You were very active in the discussion boards. It looks like you responded to at least one student every single day and you posted responses to students dozens of times each week.
- I like that you posted a weekly overview announcement every Monday to remind students of the expectations for the week.
- You offered very thorough feedback when you graded assignments. I especially enjoyed looking at the feedback you offered on the lesson plans. In that feedback, you gave specifics about areas of strength and suggestions for improving the lessons.
- The weekly videos in which you demonstrated the use of an assistive technology tool were a good enhancement to the course. I imagine students can find videos of these tools online, but seeing you use the assistive technology likely helped students connect with the learning content.

Areas for Improvement

- From looking at student assignment submissions and your grading of those submissions, I noticed that a lot of your students did not seem to understand how to include assistive technology in the IEP. I suggest you reteach this content to this cohort of students in a future course and consider adding an example IEP to this course for students to see.

> **Textbox 7.1 (Continued)**
>
> - The first week of the course had a lot of reading for students to complete! I recommend that you consider reducing those readings.
> - I noticed that there was a student question in the Q&A discussion board that you never answered. Be sure to answer all student questions.
>
> **Additional Comments:** I really enjoyed reviewing your course. From what I see, you have a strong relationship with your students and know your content well. You keep the students engaged in learning and offer valuable feedback to support their continued understanding of the content. Good work!

forgotten to respond to a student question and that the peer reviewer will notice her imperfections.

The use of peer observations of teaching can enhance faculty's reflective practices on their own instruction (Barrios-Rodríguez et al., 2023) and increase instructional effectiveness (Esterhazy et al., 2021). Beyond an increase in self-reflection and teaching skills, the use of peer reviews of teaching has other benefits to individual faculty, as well as to the university as a whole. According to Godbout-Kinney and Watson (2022), peer review of teaching reduces the bias that often occurs in student evaluations, thus making peer reviews a more accurate assessment of instructor effectiveness. The use of peer reviews encourages dialogue between faculty members who may otherwise not have the opportunity to work together; this interaction increases community building among university faculty (Donnelli-Sallee, 2018). Essentially, the research tells us that the use of peer reviews of faculty teaching is an effective practice that supports both the professor and the university.

Marla recently had the opportunity to conduct a peer review of a colleague's teaching. She really enjoyed peeking into his course and learning some new teaching practices he uses. By conducting this peer review, Marla observed that her colleague posts direct links to the textbook and videos to watch for the week in his Monday morning announcement to students. It had never occurred to her to do this, but now she includes this in her own courses as one additional method for supporting student learning.

2 Student Assessments

We mentioned in the myths section of this chapter that student evaluations are not accurate forms of assessing our teaching, but valuable information can be found in those evaluations. Similarly, we can learn a lot about our teaching effectiveness by looking at the work our students submit and comparing their work to what we are expecting to see. If we are doing our jobs as teachers, our students should be learning the content we are seeking to teach. While student work is generally not used to assess teaching quality, it is a valid way to evaluate the effectiveness of teaching and the alignment of instruction and assessment (Joyce et al., 2018). In Chapter 5, we discussed designing authentic assessments that support students in gaining, and practicing, the skills necessary for success in the PK–12 classroom. And in Chapter 6 we shared strategies for designing rubrics that evaluate student work. In order to use student assignments as part of our own self-reflection on teaching, it is vital that those assignments are well designed, accurately evaluated, and aligned with our course learning objectives.

Over the years, we have learned that every group of students is slightly different, and different supports may be needed for some cohorts of learners. Marla teaches Introduction to Special Education every semester—at this point, she has taught more than thirty sections of the course! For the most part, she feels confident that she has designed a high-quality learning experience that meets the needs of her learners. Her students tend to meet expectations on the assignments, and she consistently receives positive feedback from them about their learning. So she was shocked last fall when a large number of the students did not meet expectations on an assignment in which they were asked to write standards-based SMART individualized education program (IEP) goals. She immediately knew that she needed to figure out why and began looking at her instruction and the errors students were making. Through this self-reflection and evaluation of her own teaching, she discovered that this specific cohort of students came into the course with preconceived ideas of what IEP goals are supposed to look like and followed what they already knew instead of what the course presented to them. She retaught the concepts and specifically explained why some common patterns of IEP goal writing may be used by school districts but are not necessarily best practices. By looking at student work and self-reflecting, Marla was able to discover gaps in her instruction and better support student learning in the course.

When we use student assignments as aspects of our own teaching evaluations, there are several questions we ask ourselves as outlined in Textbox 7.2. Collectively, these questions help us answer the ultimate question: Is my instruction effectively teaching what I intend to teach to this specific group of students?

3 Professional Development

Just as PK–12 teachers are required to attend professional development (PD) opportunities to keep their certification, we as higher education faculty should also make sure we are attending to PD in all areas of teaching, but especially in online teaching. Generally, faculty are evaluated in three areas—teaching, service, and scholarship. One way that some universities want you to demonstrate good teaching is through participation in professional development opportunities. And, even if your university does not require it,

---

Textbox 7.2

Questions to Consider When Using Student Work to Evaluate Teaching

- What are the course learning objectives?
- Which of those objectives are assessed in this assignment?
- At what proficiency level do students need to demonstrate mastery of those objectives in this assignment?
- What percentage of the students are demonstrating mastery at that proficiency level?
- What percentage of the students are not demonstrating mastery at that proficiency level?
- What portion(s) of the assignment are the majority (or all) of the students doing correctly?
- What common errors are students making on this assignment?
- How have I taught those concepts that are causing errors?
- In what ways can/should I reteach those concepts?

professional development on topics related to effective online instruction can support your self-reflection practices.

One method for professional learning is the use of professional learning communities, or PLCs. Tocco et al. (2023) discuss a PLC of higher education faculty (from across a university, not just education professors) who participated in a year-long PLC focused on effective teaching in higher education. They found that participants increased their self-reflection on teaching, identified areas for professional growth, and set goals for that growth. Similarly, Gallardo-Williams and Chapman (2024) facilitated a higher education PLC that included readings, guest speakers, and discussions among faculty across the university.

There are a variety of ways that you can access professional development on online learning, some more formal than others. If your university offers professional development on online learning, we highly recommend that you participate and learn together with your colleagues. But don't let your professional development end there. Seek out other opportunities. The Online Learning Consortium (OLC) offers fantastic live and on-demand webinars on a variety of topics of interest to online teaching faculty. There are many fantastic books on the topic—see our list of suggested resources in Appendix H. And you likely have friends and colleagues who are also teaching online—tap into their knowledge. Kathy and Marla often participate in book studies on effective teaching with trusted colleagues. They have found that hand-selecting their PLC group ensures a positive learning experience and makes everyone feel more comfortable being honest in self-reflection.

As you engage in professional development in online teaching, just remember that you must take what you are learning and consider how it will support your own teaching. You must self-reflect on what you are currently doing and make changes accordingly. Professional development simply for the sake of professional development does not help you or your students.

4 Seek Out Mentors

It is likely that in your teacher preparation program, you have mentor teachers assigned to each teacher candidate. These people support the ongoing learning and professional growth of aspiring and new teachers. Similarly, we as teacher educators can benefit from having mentors. Chitpin (2010) shares her personal experience with having a mentor teacher educator; she reports that the conversations and advice she received from her mentor improved her teaching skills as evidenced in a course she was teaching. Cordie et al. (2020) note that co-teaching courses, with one very experienced instructor and a second less experienced instructor, can be an effective form of teaching mentorship in the university classroom. While we agree that this is an ideal scenario, we also realize it is not always possible due to university financial constraints or other logistical reasons. Research (Montgomery et al., 2014; van der Weijden et al., 2015) indicates that university faculty demonstrate improvements in scholarship and other job requirements as a result of structured mentorship—it stands to reason that similar results may occur for teaching-focused mentorship.

Because you are seeking to grow your skills in online teacher preparation, we highly recommend that you seek out a mentor who has significant experience with online teaching and who is considered stellar in remote instruction. In order to find this person, you may need to look outside your university. Textbox 7.3 offers a list of questions to consider when selecting

---

Textbox 7.3

Questions When Selecting a Mentor

- What are my goals for this mentorship relationship?
- What specific online teaching expertise am I looking for in a mentor?
- How much time am I hoping my mentor will dedicate to supporting my professional growth?
- How important is it to me that my mentor is at my university?
- How important is it to me that my mentor teaches the same (or similar) courses that I teach?
- What power imbalances exist (if any) with the potential mentors I am considering?
- What could be the implications on my career if there are challenges or misunderstandings in the mentorship relationship?
- What are the unique benefits to each potential mentor I am considering?

an online teaching mentor. It is important to note that, in some cases, you may want to have multiple mentors that can support various aspects of your professional development.

5 Watch Yourself Teaching

In Chapter 6, we talked about having students watch their own teaching videos. This strategy is also effective for us. We do recognize that many online courses are asynchronous, but even in classes with no required class attendance, many faculty record video lectures and offer optional live Q&A sessions, which may be recorded. While watching ourselves teach is not a comfortable feeling for many (Kathy actually despises watching herself on video), it is a vital component of reflective teaching. We need to observe our own actions in the online classroom and look at how our students are acting during our classes. When we watch ourselves teaching, we can see student behaviors, our speech patterns, our eye contact and other mannerisms, and other things that occur. Then we make changes accordingly. We have created a list of questions, found in Textbox 7.4, that we ask ourselves when observing videos of our courses. Many of the questions are similar to those we have students ask themselves when watching their own teaching videos. The reality is that our own self-reflection process should closely mirror the self-reflection process in which our students engage.

6 Making Plans for Improvement During the Course

In addition to the strategies listed above, online teacher educators should write down notes for course changes throughout the course. Many of us teach the same course every year (or possibly each semester). This means that we have many opportunities to improve our courses. Since no course is ever perfect, there is always room to improve our classes. Paul and West (2018) developed a tool for engaging in self-reflection while teaching, known as the Real-Time Instructor Observing Tool (RIOT). This tool is freely available online, and we highly recommend checking it out and using it in one of your online courses. The information gathered through using this tool can help you as you analyze and self-reflect on your own online instruction.

Kathy has a running list for each course she teaches that she uses during her virtual class meetings. On each list, she makes notes about things that need to be updated the next time the course is taught, as well as immediate updates

Textbox 7.4

Questions for Faculty Reflection on Teaching

Questions to Ask Before Watching the Video Recording

1. What was the learning objective of the lesson I was teaching?
2. How does that learning objective align with my university program learning outcomes (PLOs)? Are there any specific PLOs regarding the content being taught?
3. How does the learning objective align with my state teacher preparation standards? What specific standard(s) are aligned with this lecture?
4. To what extent were my students engaged in the lesson? What clues did I see that show me their level of engagement?
5. Based on the questions students asked, what was unclear in my instruction?
6. What do I feel went well in my instruction?
7. What do I feel did not go well in my lesson?

Questions to Ask After Watching the Video Recording

1. What are the top three things I observed myself doing well in this video?
2. What are the top three things I observed myself doing in this video that could use improvement?
3. What did I notice when viewing the video that I had not observed when I taught the lesson?
4. Based on what I noticed, what adjustments should I make to my teaching for these students in the future?
5. What else should I think about or note for myself?

or clarifications she can make to support the students currently enrolled in the course. She writes notes on assignment updates, ways to update a rubric, the need for assignment samples or better clarification on a specific learning topic, and anything else that comes up when speaking with students. She is able to use real-time student feedback to identify areas for improvement in her courses and then make immediate plans for improving those areas for the current students, as well as for students who take the course in the future. Additionally, Kathy is lucky to be able to work with instructional coaches for many of her large graduate courses. These instructional coaches do much of the grading. After working with some of them for several years, she asks input from them on things that may need to be tweaked. Since they are in the thick of grading, they have a chance to see what areas are not working, especially in final projects, and things that may need to be adjusted in the rubrics. They discuss these anytime something glaring comes up, and a note is made to make the changes. She has even had them help her revise major projects in some courses, because she is lucky enough to have some of them as adjuncts too!

Avoid This

As much as we tell you the things you *should* be doing when teaching online, we know that we can also learn from hearing what *not* to do when it comes to online teaching. These are ideas that we, or colleagues of ours, have learned the hard way to avoid.

1 Not engaging in reflection

It may seem silly to say, but the biggest "avoid this" in terms of self-reflection is choosing not to engage in reflection. In our experience, it is not uncommon for teacher educators to skip this step in teaching. We are busy, and self-reflection is hard (and often discouraging to see our own flaws). Don't make this mistake. Be intentional about scheduling time each semester to self-reflect on your instruction. Make reflection part of your teaching routine.

Figure 7.1 Reflection Process.

2 Not using reflection to guide instruction

It goes without saying (but we are going to say it anyway)—self-reflection is only useful and improves your teaching if you use that self-reflection to make changes to your course. Reflection that is not followed up with action is an ineffective teaching practice that frankly wastes a lot of time! We noted above that Wlodarsky (2005) mentions that reflection leads to increased awareness of our own teaching. This is important, but our work does not stop there. We have to reflect on our teaching, become aware of our own instructional strengths and weaknesses, and make changes based on what we have learned (see Figure 7.1).

3 Overcriticizing your own teaching

In Chapter 4, we talked about the importance of teaching your students to not be overly critical of their own teaching in remote observations—that same advice applies to ourselves when we reflect on our online instruction. Don't be overly critical of yourself—you are not perfect and are not expected to be! And, if it makes you feel better, both Kathy and Marla are very critical of their own teaching. Avoiding being overcritical of ourselves is an area of growth for both of us. Remember that it is going to take time to become effective online instructors and, even after years of doing so, we will still have significant room for growth. Give yourself grace when you reflect on your teaching.

Let's Practice—"We Do"

Professor Phiri is entering his seventh year at a teaching university and primarily teaches online courses. He is a tenured associate professor who consistently receives high-scoring teaching evaluations. His university requires self-evaluations of teaching when faculty apply for promotions, but at no other time. Professor Phiri is still several years away from his next promotion, so he is not required to reflect on his instruction. But he wants to become a more effective professor and is working to develop a professional development plan for himself. He knows that improving his teaching skills will require time and effort in his work week, which may reduce the time he has available to engage in some service and scholarship opportunities.

Now it is time to practice. This is the "We Do" part of good teaching. Answer the questions in Textbox 7.5 using the blank spaces provided. Once you have your

---

Textbox 7.5

1 Professor Phiri's dean is encouraging him not to "waste time" on reflection about his teaching but instead to focus on scholarship. Help Professor Phiri articulate to his dean why this work is vital and worthy of his time.

2 Professor Phiri knows that some of his colleagues are using teaching practices with which he is unfamiliar. He would like to observe a few colleagues' online courses. Help him craft an email to his colleagues requesting the opportunity to observe their asynchronous online courses.

3 After engaging in self-reflection, Professor Phiri has identified that he needs to improve his own skills in the area of effective student feedback. What resources would you recommend to help him learn more about giving high-quality feedback on student assignments?

answers, share them on social media using the hashtag #OnlineTeacherPrep and tagging us. You may also take a look at the suggestions included in Appendix A if you get stumped (or need a little validation that you know what you are doing).

Apply to Your Own Courses—"You Do"

It is now your time to practice being a reflective online instructor. Take time to carefully consider the questions in Textbox 7.6 as they apply to your own reflective practices.

Textbox 7.6

1. How do you feel about self-reflection on your own teaching? What excites you about being a reflective online instructor? What scares you?

2. Consider your previous online instruction. How did you evaluate your own teaching? Was the method effective? Why or why not? What did you learn about your instructional practices? What changes (if any) did you make based on what you learned?

3. Based on what you know about your own instruction, what are your instructional strengths? What are your instructional weaknesses?

(Continued)

> **Textbox 7.6 (Continued)**
>
> 4 Develop an action plan that includes a minimum of 3 steps for improving your own classroom teaching in 1 area of instructional weakness.
>
> 5 Create a step-by-step plan for increasing your self-reflective practices as an online teacher educator over the next semester. Be sure that your plan includes specific actions you will take and a timeline for completing each action.
>
> **Congratulations!**—You have now begun the process of reflecting on your teaching practices. Use what you have learned to make changes to your course or teaching as needed.

References

Barrios-Rodríguez, R., Salcedo-Bellido, I., Jiménez-Moleón, J. J., Lozano-Lorca, M., Galiano-Castillo, N., José Cobos, E., Dámaso Vílchez Rienda, J., Olmedo-Requena, R., Amezcua-Prieto, C., Martín-Peláez, S., González Domenech, C. M., Arrebola Moreno, J. P., Rica, R. A., García-Rubiño, M. E., & Requena, P. (2023). Peer review of teaching: Using the nominal group technique to improve a program in a university setting with no previous experience. *International Journal for Academic Development, 28*(4), 385–397.

Chitpin, S. (2010). Can mentoring and reflection cause change in teaching practice? A professional development journey of a Canadian teacher educator. *Professional Development in Education, 37*(2), 225–240. https://doi.org/10.1080/19415257.2010.531625

Cordie, L. A., Brecke, T., Lin, X., & Wooten, M. C. (2020). Co-teaching in higher education: Mentoring as faculty development. *International Journal of Teaching and Learning in Higher Education, 32*(1), 149–158.

Dana, H., Morrisette, S., & Nelson, S. (2023). Post-secondary student evaluations of teachers: The debate of usefulness continues. *Journal of Education and Learning, 12*(3), 54–61.

Donnelli-Sallee, E. (2018). Supporting online teaching effectiveness at scale: Achieving efficiency and effectiveness through peer review. *Journal of Educators Online, 15*(3).

Ellis, L., Burke, D. M., Lomire, P., & MacCormack, D. R. (2003). Student grades and average ratings of instructional quality: The need for adjustment. *Journal of Educational Research, 97*(1), 35–40.

Esterhazy, R., de Lange, T., Bastiansen, S., & Wittek, A. L. (2021). Moving beyond peer review of teaching: A conceptual framework for collegial faculty development. *Review of Educational Research, 91*(2), 237–271.

Felkey, A. J., & Batz-Barbarich, C. (2021). Can women teach math (and be promoted)? A meta-analysis of gender differences across student evaluations of teaching. *AEA Papers & Proceedings, 111*, 184–189. https://doi.org/10.1257/pandp.20211125

Gallardo-Williams, M. T., & Chapman, D. D. (2024). Faculty peer-to-peer learning and support online during difficult times: Main types of interactions and engagement during structured faculty conversations. *To Improve the Academy: A Journal of Educational Development, 43*(1), Article 7. https://doi.org/10.3998/tia.4052

Godbout-Kinney, K., & Watson, G. P. L. (2022). Institutional approaches to evaluate teaching effectiveness: The role of summative peer review of teaching for promotion and tenure. *Canadian Journal of Educational Administration and Policy, 201*, 2–14.

Heffernan, T. (2022). Sexism, racism, prejudice, and bias: A literature review and synthesis of research surrounding student evaluations of courses and teaching. *Assessment & Evaluation in Higher Education, 47*(1), 144–154. https://doi.org/10.1080/02602938.2021.1888075

Heffernan, T. (2023). Abusive comments in student evaluations of courses and teaching: The attacks women and marginalised academics endure. *Higher Education: The International Journal of Higher Education Research, 85*(1), 225–239. https://doi.org/10.1007/s10734-022-00831-x

Hodges, C. B., & Fowler, D. J. (2020). The COVID-19 crisis and faculty members in higher education: From emergency remote teaching to better teaching through reflection. *International Journal of Multidisciplinary Perspectives in Higher Education, 5*(1), 118–122.

Irvine, J. (2022). Relationship between teaching experience and teacher effectiveness: Implications for policy decisions. *Journal of Instructional Pedagogies, 22*, 1–19.

Joyce, J., Gitomer, D. H., & Iaconangelo, C. J. (2018). Classroom assignments as measures of teaching quality. *Learning and Instruction, 54*, 48–61. https://doi.org/10.1016/j.learninstruc.2017.08.001

Kini, T., & Podolsky, A. (2016). *Does teaching experience increase teacher effectiveness? A review of the research.* Palo Alto, CA: Learning Policy Institute. https://learningpolicyinstitute.org/our-work/publications-resources/does-teaching-experience-increase-teacher-effectiveness-review-research

Montgomery, B. L., Dodson, J. E., & Johnson, S. M. (2014). Guiding the way: Mentoring graduate students and junior faculty for sustainable academic careers. *Sage Open, 4*(4). https://doi.org/10.1177/2158244014558043

Paul, C., & West, E. (2018). Using the Real-Time Instructor Observing Tool (RIOT) for reflection on teaching practice. *Physics Teacher, 56*(3), 139–143.

Podolsky, A., Kini, T., & Darling-Hammond, L. (2019). Does teaching experience increase teacher effectiveness? A review of US research. *Journal of Professional Capital and Community, 4*(4), 286–308. https://doi.org/10.1108/JPCC-12-2018-0032

Smith, B. E., & Hawkins, B. (2011). Examining student evaluations of Black college faculty: Does race matter? *Journal of Negro Education, 80*(2), 149–162.

Stroebe, W. (2016). Why good teaching evaluations may reward bad teaching: On grade inflation and other unintended consequences of student evaluations. *Perspectives on Psychological Science, 11*(6), 800–816.

Tocco, A. J., Mehrhoff, L. A., Osborn, H. M., McCartin, L. F., & Jameson, M. M. (2023). Learning communities promote pedagogical metacognition in higher education faculty. *To Improve the Academy: A Journal of Educational Development, 42*(1), 224–254. https://doi.org/10.3998/tia.2044

Tucker, B. (2014). Student evaluation surveys: Anonymous comments that offend or are unprofessional. *Higher Education, 68*(3), 347–358. https://doi.org/10.1007/s10734-014-9716-2

van der Weijden, I., Belder, R., van Arensbergen, P., & van den Besselaar, P. (2015). How do young tenured professors benefit from a mentor? Effects on management, motivation and performance. *Higher Education, 69*, 275–287. https://doi.org/10.1007/s10734-014-9774-5

Wlodarsky, R. (2005). The professoriate: Transforming teaching practices through critical reflection and dialogue. *Teaching and Learning: The Journal of Natural Inquiry & Reflective Practice, 19*(3), Article 3. https://commons.und.edu/tl-nirp-journal/vol19/iss3/3

8 Creating a Work-Life Balance When You Are Always Connected

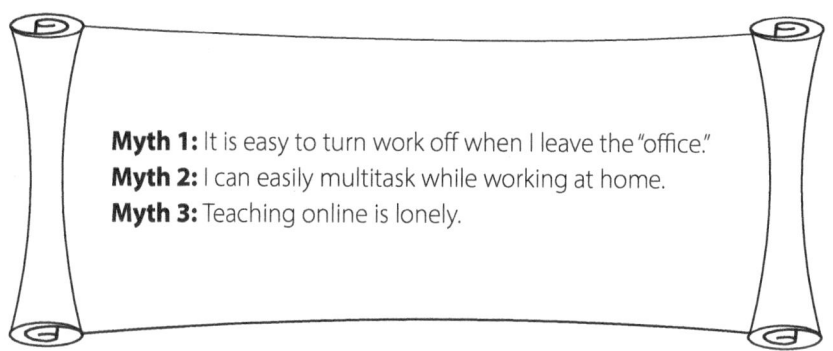

Myth 1: It is easy to turn work off when I leave the "office."
Myth 2: I can easily multitask while working at home.
Myth 3: Teaching online is lonely.

Introduction

Burnout among teachers is real and is not just occurring in PK–12 schools. Burnout leading to professionals leaving the field also occurs in higher education (Boothe & Lohmann, 2024; Jaremka et al., 2020; Khan et al., 2019; Sabagh et al., 2018). Each of you is likely experiencing some level of burnout and working with colleagues who are considering leaving the field. We do not want to become just another statistic of teacher burnout; we want to be able to continue doing what we love and for you to do the same. This chapter will focus on ways to create a work-life balance that works for you, but first we must debunk some common myths about teaching online and/or working remotely.

Online teaching can be challenging for many university faculty members (Kebritchi et al., 2017). In our experience, a large number of teacher educators consider online teaching to be more difficult and less rewarding than traditional face-to-face instruction. Many people believe that as an online instructor you can easily turn off your work when you leave. However, living in such a "connected society," this is more difficult than you may imagine. We have phone applications for our learning management systems (LMSs), our emails can be read on almost any device, and many of us carry our phones with us everywhere, which means texts and calls can come to us at any time. The other reality we are facing is that our online students are most likely taking classes due to busy work and life schedules, so they may be working on classwork at all times of the day and night. This means that you likely feel that you need to be available at different times of the day, or even be connected more often, to meet your students' needs. As much as you do not want to be "on call" 24/7, it is important to find times to meet with students and answer email and phone calls when your students are working on their schoolwork, which is likely going to be outside of traditional 8–5 work hours.

A second myth we have heard is that working from home allows for plenty of multitasking. We hear colleagues say, "This semester, I am only teaching online courses and plan to mostly work from home, so I am going to finally catch up on laundry, my family will eat good meals every night, and I am going to train for the marathon I have always wanted to run." When we hear this, we laugh a bit! Online teaching does allow for more flexibility, but it is still work and still requires full-time dedication and focus. Not going to campus will save you the daily commute time, so you may be able to do more housework and exercise more. However, it is not going to be easy, and you will have to be intentional in order to accomplish your personal and professional goals.

We recommend that you avoid plans to multitask. Kathy has recently attended a meeting with a colleague who was walking on the treadmill during the meeting. She quickly noticed two problems with this. First, it was distracting to other meeting attendees to watch the walker bouncing up and down on the screen as he walked. And, secondly, the walker was not fully engaged in the meeting, and the other meeting attendees had to repeat themselves several times. So, while well intentioned, the plan to exercise and work simultaneously was not effective. Similarly, Marla has tried to fold laundry while attending a state department of education information session. When the meeting ended, she had a stack of folded laundry to put away but struggled to articulate what she had heard in the meeting.

There has been a lot of research over the past few decades regarding multitasking. For the most part, the literature indicates that humans are not designed for multitasking, and attempting to do so makes us ineffective. Research (e.g., Bellur et al., 2015; Lee et al., 2012; Mercimek et al., 2020) found that multitasking reduces learning; we cannot learn as much information when we are not completely focused on learning. Because teaching and learning are so closely linked, and effective teaching involves constant learning, multitasking will impact teaching effectiveness. A recent study (Xu et al., 2021) on multitasking when working from home found that high-interactive multitasking, such as attending to the needs of others in the household or responding to phone calls or unexpected visitors, has a negative impact on work productivity, as these activities require greater cognitive engagement than do low-interactive multitasking activities such as folding laundry. From our own experiences and the research on multitasking, we believe that multitasking while teaching online is a myth.

The final myth we commonly hear about work-life balance when teaching online is that it is lonely and isolating. We argue that the reality of academia is that the work can be lonely regardless of whether you are on campus or online. So much of our work, including teaching courses, is independent work. We have both known several education professors who spend 10–12 hours per day on campus, arriving early and immediately going to their offices, where they shut the door and remain working alone all day. These folks bring their own lunch, which they heat up in the microwave they have in their office, and even have their personal coffee maker behind their desk—they only leave their office to use the restroom. On the flip side, we have known several online professors (ourselves included) who have used the virtual environment to build connections with professional colleagues across the country and actually feel more connected to others than we did when we worked in more traditional positions. In our experience, online faculty have ample opportunities to connect with others, if they choose to do so. Each of us has been teaching fully online and/or been remote faculty members for almost a decade—many times we find that it can be a lonesome endeavor, if we allow it to be. But we have also found that being intentional with scheduling meetings with colleagues and working from coffee shops on occasion reduces that feeling.

The research surrounding remote work, especially in terms of the social implications, is still emerging, and more recent research (post-COVID-enforced remote work) has findings that differ in some ways from the previous research on working online. The data we have seen is encouraging and aligns with what we have personally experienced—online teaching does not need to be isolating or lonely work! Schertlie et al. (2024) state that remote work can increase opportunities for workplace belonging and feelings of inclusion within a team of colleagues. And Tapani et al. (2022) found that remote work in higher education can lead to feelings of isolation and loneliness, but this can be mitigated through intentional and high-quality interactions between online faculty members and other colleagues.

Tools to Use—"I Do"

We included this chapter in the book because we wholeheartedly believe that teaching online and/or being remote faculty can be a hard challenge that most people are unprepared for when they begin online teaching. By creating a healthy work-life balance, you are taking care of yourself, so that you can be a better teacher, spouse, parent, etc. It is also a good way to model this skill to those around you (e.g., students, kids, etc.). The suggestions below will offer you ideas on creating a work-life balance that works for you and your lifestyle. We would also love to hear more about how you create a work-life balance. Please share on social media and with your colleagues so that we can continue to build our online teaching toolboxes. Please remember to use the hashtag #OnlineTeacherPrep and tag both of us in your post.

1 Have Scheduled Work Times

The most important thing we believe you can do for yourself is to have set work times that are tailored to your unique situation. Setting specific and scheduled work times has been found to be an effective way to overcome burnout (Boothe & Lohmann, 2024; Sandoval-Reyes et al., 2021). One of the benefits to online teaching is that these work times don't have to be the traditional 8–5 workday but can instead reflect the unique needs of your family and the needs of your students. When Marla first became an online professor, she had four children under the age of eight and a husband who frequently traveled for work. Due to the flexibility inherent in her job, she chose to be a work-at-home mom with paid childcare just one day per week. On the day she had childcare, she scheduled all meetings and tried to complete the work tasks that required the most focused time. On the other days, she worked for ninety minutes each morning before the children awoke, ninety minutes during naptime, and then for several hours after bedtime each evening. She also worked for two hours on Saturday mornings before her children woke up. Because all of her students worked full time and most also had young children, she scheduled student meetings beginning at 8 p.m. each evening. Her work times closely aligned with the times her students were doing their coursework.

In our experience, many faculty schedule class sessions, office hours, and meetings, but leave the rest of their calendar open for just completing tasks. We recommend being more strategic than this and scheduling all tasks into your calendar. In his book *How to Write a Lot*, Paul Silva (2018) talks about putting nonnegotiable writing appointments with yourself on your calendar. We have found this strategy to be incredibly effective for not just writing but other tasks as well. We schedule times on our calendars for course prep, grading, paperwork, writing/research, service work, and our own professional development. As suggested by Silva (2018), we treat these times as meetings that cannot be rescheduled or skipped unless an emergency arises. To keep herself from being invited to impromptu meetings by colleagues, Marla often puts herself in a Zoom meeting alone. During the writing of this book, Kathy and Marla had weekly Zoom meetings in which they both wrote independently for most of the meeting.

Scheduling your workdays and the work time within those days allows you to complete your work and find time for leisure. Figure 8.1 provides an example calendar in which we have scheduled work times and preferred activities. You will notice that our sample calendar does not have every hour of every day filled with tasks. This is intentional. When you schedule your workday, you need to leave space for "putting out fires" and for managing daily tasks such as emails and student support. Leaving empty space in your calendar also provides wiggle room for completing tasks that take longer than expected and for completing unexpected tasks that arise.

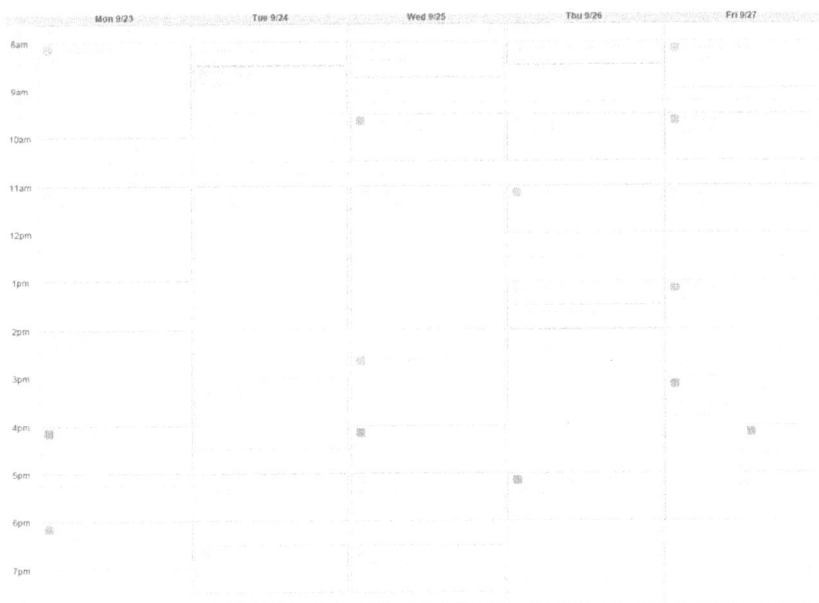

Figure 8.1 Example Schedule.

2 Be Intentional and Say "No" When Needed

Our second piece of advice is the one that both Kathy and Marla will admit is our biggest weakness in our work-life balance. We all have to learn to say no. Almost daily, we are offered professional opportunities and must make decisions about how to respond. Some of these opportunities are job requirements (e.g., serving on university committees), while others are simply part of being a responsible and contributing member of the academic community (e.g., serving as a journal peer reviewer). We are not advocating turning down any of these required opportunities. Instead, our advice is to be strategic in your responses to optional professional opportunities. This can be especially difficult when the opportunity for a cool project comes along or when your favorite colleagues ask you to work on something with them. But sometimes we have to say no to enticing opportunities. When a professional opportunity arises, ask yourself the questions outlined in Textbox 8.1 (and we suggest asking them in the order listed).

Be intentional about "life" time and communicate this to students/colleagues. Your students need to know you are real and also have to work and have a life outside of your career. Let your students know your time constraints.

> **Textbox 8.1**
>
> **Questions to Ask When Opportunities Arise**
>
> 1. Is this something that I am required to do in order to complete my job requirements?
> 2. Is this something I need to do in order to be a contributing member of my academic community?
> 3. Is this something that I have time to complete and can complete to a standard that I will be happy with?
> 4. Is this something that I want to do? Does this opportunity excite me?
> 5. What are the professional benefits to saying yes?
> 6. What are the personal and professional drawbacks to saying yes?

For example, if you are going out of town and will not be around as much, let them know. If you need to cancel class, let them know. Because she teaches year-round with no breaks between the end of one course and the start of the next, Kathy goes on vacation during courses she is teaching and occasionally will go on a cruise with limited wifi access. When this happens, she intentionally plans for it by communicating early to students and planning coursework that students can complete with little or no support during her absence. Marla strongly values church and family time and does not work on Sundays; she tells students this from the first day of every course and is diligent about not logging into her courses or responding to student emails, texts, or phone calls on Sundays (unless a student texts or calls about a true emergency).

3 Designated Work Space

Thirdly, we suggest having a dedicated work space within your home. During COVID, the majority of workers worked from home, and one of the most frequent pieces of advice we saw was the importance of having a dedicated work space. In our experience, that is a vital practice for ensuring work-life balance. A recent study (Xiao et al., 2021) found that remote workers without a dedicated work space have a higher likelihood of developing mental health concerns, specifically stress and anxiety, related to their work environment.

A designated work space does not necessarily have to be a home office but can be anyplace you choose to work. Regardless of where you choose as your designated work space, you want to ensure you have what you need. Make sure you have access to the internet, your textbooks, journal articles, audio/video recording tools, paper, pens/pencils, etc.

As a busy mom of four, Marla has found that having a dedicated home office is vital for focused work time, video meetings, and for storing/organizing all her work materials, but that she also needs a mobile "office space" as well. She keeps a laptop bag packed at all times with pens, notepaper, and Post-It notes. Before taking kids to activities almost every evening, she grabs the bag and puts her laptop inside. She is known for using her mobile office at the soccer field on Tuesday nights, the high school parking lot for theater practice on Wednesdays, the coffee shop next door to gymnastics on Thursdays, and the pool deck all summer. In addition, she frequently works from the mobile office in the car pickup line in the afternoons. Marla has learned (the hard way) that it is important to restock the mobile office on a regular basis and be diligent about keeping her laptop charged in preparation for packing it in the mobile office. It is important to note that Marla's remote office is not a strategy for overworking. Because she wants to be fully present for her children, her traditional workday ends when her children's school day ends. She works while they are engaged in activities in the evenings as a trade-off for the time she spends with her children after school.

4 Make Time for Yourself

Next, we recommend making time for self-care. Over the past several years, we have noticed that this term gets thrown around a lot. That is for good reason. Self-care occurs when people intentionally care for their own needs in order to prevent physical or mental illness (Riegel et al., 2021). The National Institute of Mental Health (2024) recommends self-care activities such as (a) regular exercise, (b) healthy eating, (c) staying hydrated, (d) getting enough sleep, (e) making time for preferred activities, and (f) staying connected with others.

O'Dwyer et al. (2018) published a poem reminding academics about the importance of caring for oneself, both inside and outside of the academy. We highly recommend their poem as a reminder of the value of self-care.

Clearly, the research tells us that we must engage in self-care (and most of us know that without being told to do so). Because we know it is important, it should be easy to make time for yourself, right? Sadly, we have found that is not always the case. And teaching remotely can make it even harder due to the easy access to "the office" and our work. Many online instructors feel like they need to be "on" at all times of the day and night for their students, but we must stop doing this. We will not be effective instructors if we are not taking care of ourselves.

There are so many activities that you can do to care for yourself. We talked earlier in this chapter about scheduling your work time. It is also important that you schedule specific time in your calendar—daily, weekly, monthly—to take care of you. Some great ways to take care of yourself would be to take a spa day (or even just a massage or facial), take an hour to work out, get some meditation in, enjoy the sun, take a brisk walk by the water, listen to music, go to a movie, or get creative with a hobby such as ceramics. The list goes on and on. Many of these activities, among others, release what are known as happiness chemicals (e.g., serotonin, dopamine, endorphins, oxytocin) (Watson, 2024). This means that when we are engaged in certain activities like those discussed above, as well as many others, we are releasing chemicals in our body that ultimately make us happier. Happiness is a good thing! Happiness makes us less stressed, which means we are more productive and better at our jobs.

For our first several years as fully online faculty, we were not good at self-care. Over time, though, we have both become more intentional about making time for ourselves and our own health. Marla has discovered that she needs to be physically active in order to feel both physically and mentally healthy. With her parenting responsibilities, it can be hard to make it to the gym in the evening or on weekends, so she has learned how to build exercise into her workday. She is a runner and has discovered that a good run helps her body feel better and her brain work through issues and concerns better. One of her favorite strategies is to go for a run in the middle of a writing/research session or in the middle of course development work, right when she has hit a tough spot or question to ponder. While running, she can think through the issue and usually returns home from her run feeling physically energized and ready to move forward with her work. Kathy is definitely not a fitness person, so her self-care looks different from Marla's but works all the same. She has found that having a schedule is helpful. When creating her schedule for the day, she will schedule in time for things she enjoys such as reading (for fun), diamond painting, adult coloring, taking the dog out for a walk, and mindfulness activities. She also makes it a priority, most of the time, to stop working once her husband gets home from work.

While caring for ourselves is vital to our success as online teacher educators, it also matters for our students. We know that modeling is an effective teaching strategy (Archer & Hughes, 2011); our students learn both from the content we teach and from their observations of us. By taking care of ourselves, we are also modeling to our students the work-life balance they should strive for so that they are better for their own families and students.

5 Network

We know that stress and burnout in education are real, and one way to overcome this is to build and maintain positive relationships (Boothe & Lohmann, 2024; Boren, 2014)—in other words, FIND YOUR PEOPLE! This is the biggest piece of advice we can give. By building these relationships, we have people we can depend on and those we can ask for help if things get to be too much. Asking for help has been identified in the literature as an effective way to handle burnout (Boothe, 2024; Pietarinen et al., 2013; Tikkanen et al., 2022).

As we mentioned in the Introduction, we have supported one another as we have navigated online teaching. We have several phone calls each week to discuss challenges we are facing with our teaching, share "wins" in our classrooms, or help one another strategize about a new teaching idea we want to implement in our classrooms. In addition, we both participate in online writing retreats and virtual professional book clubs, as well as intentionally conducting research with friends at other universities.

When Marla puts together her work calendar each week, she tries to ensure that she has at least one scheduled time to connect with colleagues during the week (and often many more arise as the week progresses). Her favorite networking time is Zoom-based writing retreats, and she hosts these several times per semester for colleagues at her own university and special education colleagues across the country. These networking times always begin with a little time for small talk/catching up, followed by sharing writing goals for the day and a few hours of independent writing time before getting back together again.

Kathy connects with colleagues through writing meetings, but also through group text messages and using social media. Kathy is part of several Facebook groups related to special education and teacher preparation. She will spend time asking and answering questions that arise on those sites. She finds it is sometimes helpful to be a part of teacher groups and state groups to keep her "in the know" of what is happening in the PK–12 classrooms. She also is part of several group texts where participants discuss many topics such as world events, job advice, our families, and, of course, asking for help or suggestions on our work.

Additionally, we encourage you to get out and become part of an organization or group focused on your content area. This allows you to be with like-minded people who share your passion. We have been blessed by getting ourselves involved in the Council for Exceptional Children's (CEC) Teacher Education Division (TED) during our doctoral program. We have been involved with this organization ever since and have found our "home" in which we network. Many organizations host yearly conferences or webinars, or other types of meet and greets, in which you can meet with those familiar with your area of expertise and bounce ideas off each other. We both make it a point, as do many of our colleagues, to attend the annual conference so we can network face-to-face at least once a year and attend several online events throughout the year.

Work-Life Balance Tools

We spent the previous section discussing strategies that we implement monthly, weekly, or even daily into our schedules to help us create a solid work-life balance. Table 8.1 provides you with tools that you may find helpful with incorporating more balance into your already hectic life!

Table 8.1 Tools for Creating a Work-Life Balance

	Name	Link
Have scheduled work times	Google Calendar	https://calendar.google.com
	Calendly	https://calendly.com
Make time for yourself	Calm App	https://www.calm.com
	The Mindful App	https://www.themindfulnessapp.com
	My Fitness Pal App	https://www.myfitnesspal.com
	SpaFinder	https://www.spafinder.com
Network	Council for Exceptional Children (CEC)	https://exceptionalchildren.org
	American Educational Research Association (AERA)	https://www.aera.net
	Association of Literacy Educators and Researchers (ALER)	https://www.aleronline.org

Avoid This

While we have provided you with lots of "what to do's" and even some "what not to do's," we would be remiss if we didn't specifically state some things to avoid when it comes to creating a work-life balance.

1 Work 24/7

This is definitely difficult for many of us, but it is so important! When teaching online, it can be so easy to think, "I have five minutes. I will just sneak in a bit more work or respond to another student email." However, this approach can be counterproductive and lead to burnout and unrealistic expectations from your students of immediate responses to all their requests. You need to set boundaries and take care of yourself. Set a schedule and stick to it, take your email off your electronics so that you are not tempted to check emails, or get outside and do something you enjoy to reduce the temptation to be available to your students. Let students and colleagues know when you will be available and how long they should expect to wait for a response—and follow it!

2 Being superman/woman

You are not expected to, and cannot, do it all. And that is okay! Just as our students have outside responsibilities, we do too—remember that. We can only do so much, and just because we may not have to commute to and from work and are not teaching for three straight hours does not mean that we can do more than our colleagues, or should be expected to. Do what you can, and remember to enjoy yourself and your family and friends.

3 Staying isolated

Get out and network. This is so important. Teaching online and/or working remotely can get lonesome and boring. Find ways to stay active in both your professional and personal lives. Consider taking your remote office to a coffee shop on some days or schedule virtual co-work times with colleagues. Throughout this chapter, we have provided you some ways to stay connected while teaching online. Choose one until you find something you enjoy! You will be happier, which will show in your productivity both at work and at home.

Let's Practice—"We Do"

Professor Thompson is currently teaching 12 credit hours of asynchronous online courses and has received approval from her university dean to work fully remotely four days per week, with the requirement that she attend meetings and hold office hours on campus every Friday. She has three young children and is hoping this arrangement will offer her the opportunity to spend more time with her children and volunteer in their school on a regular basis. Currently, her oldest child is in kindergarten and attends school five days per week. Professor Thompson has enrolled the younger two children in half-day preschool on Tuesday, Wednesday, and Thursday mornings and has arranged for a full-day nanny on Fridays. She wants to ensure that she meets the needs of her students and fulfills all university obligations while making time for her family. Professor

Thompson needs to develop a plan for achieving her personal and professional goals while teaching online.

Now it is time to practice. This is the "We Do" part of good teaching. Answer the questions in Textbox 8.2 using the blank spaces provided. Once you have your answers, share them on social media using the hashtag #OnlineTeacherPrep and tagging us. You may also take a look at the suggestions provided in

Textbox 8.2

1 Identify at least three challenges Professor Thompson might experience as she attempts to create work-life balance in this situation.

2 Design a schedule that Professor Thompson might use to organize her days, while ensuring she meets both work and family obligations.

3 Draw the physical work space that you would recommend Professor Thompson create in her home.

4 Offer specific and actionable advice to Professor Thompson on achieving her goals.

Appendix A if you get stumped (or need a little validation that you know what you are doing).

Apply to Your Own Courses—"You Do"

It is now your time to practice creating a work-life balance. Follow the steps given in Textbox 8.3. Once you have completed the steps, you will have one idea ready to implement in your next online course.

> **Textbox 8.3**
>
> **1** List your work responsibilities below. Next to each responsibility, write out how long you would like to devote each week to that particular responsibility. Include times you will devote to office hours, scholarship (writing), service, and even include times you will respond to emails. Don't forget to include times when you will teach or record lectures, as well as time in your day to grade and work on updating course content.
>
> **2** Following the same process as above, do the same for your personal responsibilities. Include family time, doctor appointments, "me" time, errands, kids' extracurricular activities, etc.

(Continued)

> **Textbox 8.3 (Continued)**
>
> **3** Create a list of things you enjoy doing. What is one thing from your list that you can commit to this week? Use the space below to jot down your thoughts.
>
> **4** Identify people you can network with—even if it is one other person—and write the name(s) below. Identify a way to stay connected with them and set a schedule for that check-in. Write this below.
>
> **5** Now, take all the information you provided above and create yourself a schedule.
>
> **Congratulations!**—You just started the process of creating work-life balance in your daily life!

References

Archer, A. L., & Hughes, C. A. (2011). *Explicit instruction: Effective and efficient teaching.* Guilford Press.

Bellur, S., Nowak, K. L., & Hull, K. S. (2015). Make it our time: In class multitaskers have lower academic performance. *Computers in Human Behavior, 53*(3), 63–70. https://doi.org/10.1016/j.chb.2015.06.027

Boothe, K. A., & Lohmann, M. J. (2024). Modeling and encouraging self-care in online teacher preparation: Lessons learned during the COVID-19 pandemic. *Networks: An Online Journal for Teacher Research, 25*(1). https://doi.org/10.4148/2470-6353.1376

Boren, J. P. (2014). The relationships between co-rumination, social support, stress, and burnout among working adults. *Management Communication Quarterly, 28*(1), 3–25. https://doi.org/10.1177/0893318913509283

Jaremka, L. M., Ackerman, J. M., Gawronski, B., Rule, N. O., Sweeny, K., Tropp, L. R., Metz, M. A., Molina, L., Ryan, W. S., & Vick, S. B. (2020). Common academic experiences no one talks about: Repeated rejection, impostor syndrome, and burnout. *Perspectives on Psychological Science, 15*(3), 519–543. https://doi.org/10.1177/1745691619898848

Kebritchi, M., Lipschuetz, A., & Santiague, L. (2017). Issues and challenges for teaching successful online courses in higher education: A literature review. *Journal of Educational Technology Systems, 46*(1), 4–29. https://doi.org/10.1177/0047239516661713

Khan, A., Din, S., & Anwar, M. (2019). Sources and adverse effects of burnout among academic staff: A systematic review. *City University Research Journal, 9*(2), 350–362.

Lee, J., Lin, L., & Robertson, R. (2012). The impact of media multitasking on learning. *Learning, Media, and Technology, 37*(1), 94–104. https://doi.org/10.1080/17439884.2010.537664

Mercimek, B., Akbulut, Y., Donmez, O., & Sak, U. (2020). Multitasking impairs learning from multimedia across gifted and non-gifted students. *Educational Technology Research and Development, 68*(3), 995–1016. https://www.jstor.org/stable/48727474

National Institute of Mental Health. (2024). *Caring for your mental health.* https://www.nimh.nih.gov/health/topics/caring-for-your-mental-health

O'Dwyer, S., Pinto, S., & McDonough, S. (2018). Self-care for academics: A poetic invitation to reflect and resist. *Reflective Practice, 19*(2), 243–249. https://doi.org/10.1080/14623943.2018.1437407

Pietarinen, J., Pyhältö, K., Soini, T., & Salmela-Aro, K. (2013). Validity and reliability of the socio-contextual teacher burnout inventory (STBI). *Psychology, 4*, 73–82.

Riegel, B., Dunbar, S. B., Fitzsimons, D., Freedland, K. E., Lee, C. S., Middleton, S., Stromberg, A., Vellone, E., Webber, D. E., & Jaarsma, T. (2021). Self-care research: Where are we now? Where are we going? *International Journal of Nursing Sciences, 116*. https://doi.org/10.1016/j.ijnurstu.2019.103402.

Sabagh, Z., Hall, N. C., & Saroyan, A. (2018). Antecedents, correlates and consequences of faculty burnout. *Educational Research, 60*(2), 131–156. https://doi.org/10.1080/00131881.2018.1461573

Sandoval-Reyes, J., Idrovo-Carlier, S., & Duque-Oliva, E. J. (2021). Remote work, work stress, and work-life during pandemic times: A Latin America situation.

International Journal of Environmental Research and Public Health, 18(13), 7069. https://doi.org/10.3390/ijerph18137069

Schertler, M., Glumann, N. V., & Boehm, S. A. (2024). How two megatrends affect each other: Studying the interplay of remote work and workplace inclusion with a random intercept cross-lagged panel model. *Academy of Management Discoveries, 10*(3), 351–374.

Silva, P. J. (2018). *How to write a lot: A practical guide to productive academic writing.* APA Life Tools.

Tapani, A., Sinkkonen, M., Sjoblom, K., Vangrieken, K., & Makikangas, A. (2022). Experiences of relatedness during enforced remote work among employees in higher education. *Challenges, 13*(2). https://doi.org/10.3390/challe13020055

Tikkanen, L., Haverinen, K., Pyhältö, K., Pietarinen, J., & Soini, T. (2022). Differences in teacher burnout between schools: Exploring the effect of proactive strategies on burnout trajectories. *Frontiers in Education, 7*, Article 858896.

Watson, S. (2024). *Feel-good hormones: How they affect your mind, mood, and body.* https://www.health.harvard.edu/mind-and-mood/feel-good-hormones-how-they-affect-your-mind-mood-and-body

Xiao, Y., Becerik-Gerber, B., Lucas, G., & Roll, S. C. (2021). Impacts of working from home during COVID-19 pandemic on physical and mental well-being of office workstation users. *Journal of Occupational and Environmental Medicine, 63*(3), 181–190. https://doi.org/10.1097/JOM.0000000000002097

Xu, S., Kerk, K., & Mao, C. (2021). Multitasking and work-life balance: Explicating multitasking when working from home. *Journal of Broadcasting & Electronic Media, 65*(3), 397–425.

Conclusion

Thank you for taking the time to read this book. We hope that you have enjoyed reading it as much as we enjoyed writing it. Our wish for you as you finish your journey with this book is that you feel more prepared to support student learning in the virtual classroom and feel excited and empowered to meet the needs of your students.

Before we go, we would like to recap what we shared in each of the chapters and offer a brief introduction to each of the appendices that follow this Conclusion.

We began the book with two important aspects of online teaching. Chapter 1 looked at ways you can prepare your students and your course to help them become engaged with the course. Chapter 2 is where we discussed activities and instructional practices that help build community. Because we know that discussion boards are a common practice, Chapter 3 focused on how to create meaningful and engaging discussion boards for your students. In Chapter 4, we discussed helpful tips on remote observations, and in Chapter 5, we provided different types of authentic assessments that could be incorporated into your online courses. Chapter 6 follows along the same path of assessing student learning, but we specifically discuss ways to assess student learning. We then ended the book with Chapters 7 and 8, which focus on you, as the instructor. Chapter 7 focused on ways to become a reflective practitioner and how to use that reflection to improve your courses. The last chapter of our book, Chapter 8, shared some helpful strategies we've found for achieving a solid work-life balance.

We have also included several appendices that provide you with additional topics of importance in online teaching. As mentioned in the Introduction, and throughout the book, Appendix A is our answers to many of the "We Do" questions found in the chapters of this book. Appendix B focuses on helping you think through how you can create authentic assessments by providing specific examples of different types of authentic assessment. We know that many of our students who come to us have disabilities, including neurodiversity, and we want to provide a good education to them while also meeting their needs, so Appendix C focuses on compliance with the Americans with Disabilities Act (ADA), specifically Title II. Along those same lines, Appendix D focuses on Universal Design for Learning as a way to meet the needs of *all* your students. Appendices E and F were included to provide insight into two important aspects of teaching: trauma-informed instruction and artificial intelligence. We end the book with Appendices G and H where we provide you with a list of our favorite things to have while teaching online and additional resources we feel may help you in your online teaching.

Thank you again for reading our work. Please don't hesitate to reach out to us. And don't forget to share your success stories with us on Twitter/X. Kathy can be found at @kah1978, and Marla is at @MarlaLohmann. Please use the hashtag #OnlineTeacherPrep and tag both of us in your post.

Appendix A: "We Do" Responses from Kathy and Marla

In this appendix, we offer our own answers to some of the questions posed in the "We Do" section of each chapter. We suggest that you first consider the question being posed, create your own response to the question, and then look at our response to compare with yours. While we did not respond to all of the "We Do's" in the book, we did answer the majority of them. Most likely if we did not answer the question below, it is because we provided an example in the chapter.

Chapter 1: Engaging Learners in Teacher Education Coursework

1 In your experience, why might Professor Laurent's students not be participating in the course?

   We believe one reason Professor Laurent's students are not participating is because he has not worked to build community (see Chapter 2) in his online course, nor has he tried any strategies that could help his students engage with the coursework, such as creating a flipped classroom or using group work.

2 What immediate action can Professor Laurent take to enhance student engagement in the course? What can he do today?

   The quickest and easiest strategy Professor Laurent could do now is to create scheduled announcements. In his scheduled announcements, he could discuss with his students what they are responsible for completing that week. He could also start scheduling weekly online office hours so his students could get to know him better and ask questions that they may feel embarrassed to ask in class. He could then take these questions and discuss them in his virtual meetings.

3 What three strategies should Professor Laurent implement over the next month? What action steps does he need to take in order to implement those strategies?

Note: Many of the suggestions in this answer are also discussed in the next chapter.

Professor Laurent can implement scheduled announcements, a flipped classroom, and group work in one easy motion!

a *The first step for Professor Laurent is to review his syllabus to determine the content he will be sharing each week. At this time, he should develop 3–5 discussion questions for the students over the content being taught in the asynchronous class.*

b *Simultaneously, he could create a poll or survey for his students to determine their teaching experience, such as what grade and subject the students teach, as well as geographic location.*

c *The third step for Professor Laurent is creating scheduled announcements that he would post every Monday at 8 a.m. In the first scheduled announcement, he would be open with his students about the changes he is going to make and why. Then each of the scheduled announcements he would tell the students the expectations for the week and provide a review of the discussion questions that he will be asking in the asynchronous meeting.*

d *If he chooses to use group work during his asynchronous class, he needs to decide the best way to group his students. Once he has this information, he can complete his lecture, and when he is ready for the discussions, he can put his students into breakout sessions where they do a Think, Pair, Share activity with the discussion questions.*

If he chooses to do the group work as a discussion, he will create his groups each week through the learning management system (LMS) and provide specific criteria for what students need to accomplish each week according to the specific discussion questions he provides.

4 As Professor Laurent prepares to teach this same course again next semester, what should he be considering?

We suggest that Professor Laurent prepare to start the semester off by contacting his students, either through email or phone call, and introducing himself. Next we suggest he prepare and post information on the weekly office hours he is available to his students. If he has already worked on the steps above for some weeks, he can use the same scheduled posts to reach out to his students. For any weeks he does not already have scheduled posts, he can create them. Another thing that we have not discussed here is to choose at least 1–2 modules and find ways to vary instructional tools by providing multiple means of representing the content and by offering choice in a discussion or on the weekly/final assignment.

Chapter 2: Building Online Learning Communities

1 Why should Dr. Lopez care that students feel isolated in his course?

When students feel isolated, we may find that they feel as though they do not belong, and thus their stress levels increase, they have low levels of class engagement, and they may drop your class or the program. Dr. Lopez should care if his students feel isolated because it could have a negative impact on their learning.

2 Provide three specific practices that Dr. Lopez could use to support the learning community throughout the course.

Dr. Lopez can support learning by being active on social media and sharing his expertise with his students and others who follow him on social media. He could also provide optional meetings where he discusses the week's activities and/or lectures over the weekly or module topic. Another way Dr. Lopez could support the community in his class is by providing informal spaces for his students to meet, such as creating a student lounge or a question-and-answer discussion board.

Chapter 3: Asynchronous Discussion Boards That Enhance Student Learning

1 Select a discussion format that would be appropriate for this planned discussion and would support the students in achieving the learning objective outlined by Dr. Bullock.

An infographic would work for this scenario. In this discussion, each student could choose the technology tool they will incorporate into their lesson plan. The infographic would include information about the technology tool as well as ways it can be used for the subject/content of the lesson plan.

2 What barriers might students face in completing this discussion? How should Dr. Bullock proactively prevent those barriers?

In looking at the above infographic discussion, there are a few barriers that come to mind. One barrier is that you may have students who do not know what an infographic is or how to create one. One way to prevent this barrier is to explicitly teach this skill and/or provide additional resources that include examples and how-to videos/articles. A second barrier to infographic discussions is that some students will focus more on making the infographic look attractive than on the content itself. To combat this, ensure your rubric reflects the importance of good information in the infographic and that you explicitly tell students that you are grading on content.

3 What supports or additional information might Dr. Bullock need to give his students to be able to complete your chosen discussion format?

Dr. Bullock should provide the students with examples of an infographic. He should also ensure that students know what to include in their infographic. Finally, he should provide directions on how to create infographics. These directions should be written and in video format.

Chapter 4: Implementing Remote Observations of Field Experiences into Online Programming

1 Identify which of the four observations will be in person and which three observations will be remote. Offer a rationale for your decision.

We suggest that the third observation be in person and the first, second, and last observations be remote. By doing a remote observation first, this allows the student and the instructor a practice round to figure out everything related to recording, submitting the recording, etc. With the second observation, the student has a better understanding of the requirements and how to work everything and is becoming more familiar with being observed, as are their students. The third observation should then be done in person, as students have had time to review and begin implementing the feedback you have provided in the other two observations. You will also have a chance during this observation to possibly model any skills the student is still struggling with. The fourth and final observation can then be done as a final review to ensure the student is proficient in the specific skills you have been observing them on. If Dr. Lopez chooses, he could switch the second and third observations.

2. Identify the responsibilities of each party (Professor Ruiz, university supervisor, host school, and teacher candidate) in the remote observation process.

Professor Ruiz: Set up day and time with teacher candidate to complete face-to-face observation. Meet with student to review remote observation requirements. Review remote observations and provide feedback to teacher candidate for all 4 observations.

University Supervisor: Schedule teacher candidates to host schools. Obtain permission from the host school for recording. Be the liaison between the professor, host school, and teacher candidate.

Host School: Give permission to university supervisor for recording. Work closely with the teacher candidate to ensure adequate training and assistance. Work with the university supervisor when problems arise.

Teacher Candidate: Ensure permission has been granted for recording. Set up camera adhering to the directions provided. Submit remote observation recordings to professor.

Chapter 5: Authentic Assessment as an Instructional Practice

1. In this scenario, why is it important for Dr. Liu to design an assessment that her students can use immediately?

Dr. Liu is looking for an assessment her students can use immediately because many of them are currently working as long-term substitutes. Remember the old saying "Kill two birds with one stone"? By creating a project they can take with them into the classroom as soon as it is graded, it is taking one thing away from their plate that they would consider added work. Additionally, Dr. Liu has found that authentic assessments help her students in building specific skills related to the assessment, and her students can implement the feedback received before they have to take their school project into their daily jobs.

2 In this scenario, why is it vital that the assessment Dr. Liu creates has flexibility to meet the various student realities present in her class?

Dr. Liu likes to include flexibility in her assignments whenever possible. She does this for many reasons. One reason is that she wants her students to see how the assignments they are completing in her course relate to what they have to do in the classroom. By providing this flexibility, it does not matter what the student's major is; they can still complete the assignment and make it work for them. A second reason Dr. Liu incorporates flexibility in her assessments is so that she can proactively address student learning needs.

3 What activities can you use in helping your students understand and be able to use explicit and direct instruction in their classrooms?

After reviewing explicit and direct instruction for the class, Dr. Liu could create role plays where she has students break into groups and each student gets the chance to act as a teacher. The role-play scenarios would be of both explicit and direct instruction. The students would be able to guess which is being described in each.

Chapter 6: Assessing Student Learning

1 Describe to Dr. Liu why she needs to provide students with the rubric when giving them an assessment.

I would explain to Dr. Liu that rubrics are important to students so that they know the specifics of their grading. While many instructors have students who may not care, many other students strive for perfection, and a rubric will allow them to know how to achieve that. Additionally, by providing rubrics, students who have busy schedules will know where to focus their time for the assignment. Finally, many students get anxious when it comes to completing and submitting assignments—providing a rubric can help alleviate this stress.

2 Considering both the assessment topic and the rubric you created, consider the type of feedback that Dr. Liu should use when grading this assessment. What might be the benefits and drawbacks of written, audio, and video feedback?

Without knowing your rubric, we offer our ideas. Considering the rubric example provided in Chapter 6, we believe that written feedback should be sufficient, but we strongly encourage that the feedback be specific about what was good in the assignment and about areas the student needs to work on. One benefit of written feedback is that you could use the copy-and-paste feature on your computer, so you would not have to recreate the same statement over and over. Drawbacks to written feedback are that it can be time consuming and may be interpreted incorrectly by the student. Audio feedback has the benefit that it allows us to explicitly tell our students the good and bad of their assignment, and the students get to hear our voice, making us more "real" to them. Video feedback, on the other hand, is the most specific type of feedback, and while you can talk to your student, you can also show them where their mistakes are, how to change the mistakes, where to find information to change things, etc. Audio and video feedback both have drawbacks. Drawbacks include that you may not be able to grade on the go because you need a quiet place as well as access to a microphone and video camera. These forms of feedback may also take additional time to make them effective.

Chapter 7: The Reflective Practitioner

1 Professor Phiri's dean is encouraging him not to "waste time" on reflection about his teaching but to focus instead on scholarship. Help Professor Phiri articulate to his dean why this work is vital and worthy of his time.

Professor Phiri can start by finding a way he can incorporate his teaching into his research. If Professor Phiri can find a way to do this, he could simply talk to his dean about how he can focus on reflecting to improve his teaching and write about what he learns through this activity as a scholarship activity, or if he is really good, maybe two or three scholarship activities. We also believe it is important for Professor Phiri to discuss with his dean the pros to being a reflective practitioner.

2 Professor Phiri knows that some of his colleagues are using teaching practices with which he is unfamiliar. He would like to observe a few colleagues' online courses. Help him craft an email to his colleagues requesting the opportunity to observe their asynchronous online courses.

Dear Dr. Marla Lohmann,

As you know, there is a lot of encouragement from the university as well as recent literature that discusses the importance of peer observations to improve teaching practices. Since I am an associate professor, I am still trying to grow my skills, especially in online teaching. I have heard from students and other professors that you provide engaging and well-developed online courses. As I try to grow in my profession, I wonder if it would be possible for me to observe you in action. I teach Tuesdays at 5 p.m. and 6 p.m. and Wednesdays at 5 p.m. If you meet with any of your classes virtually outside of these times, I would love to schedule a time with you to observe. I am also wondering if you would have time to sit down with me and walk me through your syllabus and course setup so I can compare them to mine and see what I might be able to change. I know that this could be time consuming, but I can make myself available at any time and we can even meet in a few shorter meetings if needed. I value your knowledge in online teaching and your opinion. I hope you will consider one or both of my requests.

Sincerely,

Dr. Kathleen Boothe

Chapter 8: Creating a Work-Life Balance When You Are Always Connected

1 Identify at least three challenges Professor Thompson might experience as she attempts to create work-life balance in this situation.

One challenge Professor Thompson will have to deal with is the afternoons and Mondays when her two smallest are at home.

A second challenge Professor Thompson will experience is being able to volunteer on a regular basis.

A third challenge for Professor Thompson might be her having to deal with drop-off and pickup times and her work obligations such as Zoom meetings.

2 Offer specific and actionable advice to Professor Thompson on achieving her goals.

Professor Thompson could start by writing a list of everything that has to be done each day, such as dropping off and picking up children, standing meetings, days she is in the office, drive times, live classes, aerobics classes, etc. Once she has this list, she needs to determine what can be done by other people and, if needed, ask for help! She can also begin putting these items on her calendar. Once the standard appointments or activities are scheduled, she should write a list of other things that need to get done but do not have to be done at a specific time or on a specific day. Now that she has this list, she can begin to add those into her calendar where they fit. Now Professor Thompson is ready to schedule activities and other things that she would like, but it is not required, to do.

Appendix B: "You Do" Examples

We know that many of us, our students included, love to see examples of things we are asking them to do (and, as we noted in Chapter 6, exemplars are a good way to support learning). While we have done our best to give you several examples throughout the book, we also didn't want to clutter the pages of the book too much. In Chapter 5, we included a table where we provided several ideas on ways to incorporate different types of authentic assessments into your courses. However, we also know that may not be enough, and since we are such proponents of Universal Design for Learning (UDL), we thought we would take the time to provide some examples in this appendix. Not all the examples follow the guidelines we have given about being clear in your expectations, but that is because we are going for short and want to give you ideas—please note that when we use these assignments in our courses, we provide students with significant guidance in both the assessment prompt and the rubric. We hope you find these examples useful in your courses, or at the very least that they help you in brainstorming something that will work for you and your students.

Role Plays

1 In your group of three, assign everyone a role (you will need two caregivers and one teacher). Once everyone has been assigned a role, you will each get a scenario in which you need to play your assigned role as a member of the parent-teacher conference. While engaging in your role play, remember all that you have learned thus far in class.

   a *Scenario Example:* Mr. Ruelas is a 4th grade teacher in an upper middle-class school. Mr. and Mrs. Yadao are attending the midyear parent-teacher conference. They are worried that their daughter

Jasmine has not been doing well in her classes. Jasmine's parents discuss the fact that Jasmine was doing well in the previous grading period, but now she is not and they think it is Mr. Ruelas's fault. As you role play Mr. Ruelas, think about the best course of action to address this and then work with the parents to develop a plan that ensures accountability for everyone—teacher, parents, *and* student.

Newsletters

1 Prepare a beginning-of-school newsletter that you might send home to families describing your classroom. In your newsletter, you should think about everything we have touched on so far in class. This should be an actual newsletter you design—it should not just be a paragraph in a Word document. It should include color, pictures—be appealing to the eye—something families would want to read.

Your newsletter should include the following at a minimum—add as much as you would like:

  a A welcome to the class, including your name and contact information

  b Classroom rules

  c Positive/negative consequences

  d Classroom schedule (depending on level)

  e Your overall philosophy of teaching and learning—how will your class be run?

  f Any other relevant information you feel you need to include in your first communication with families.

Classroom Management System

1 The last few weeks, we have focused on Tier 1 positive behavior interventions and supports (PBIS). Now I want you to take what you have learned and create a behavior matrix, following the guidelines discussed in class. Additionally, using the behavior matrix you completed, I want you to now create your classroom rules, based on the schoolwide PBIS matrix.

2. Create a token economy for your classroom. Be sure to outline the expectations that will earn students tokens, as well as an explanation of how tokens may be spent. Consider how you will support the needs of struggling learners within this system.

Individualized Education Program

1. Use the sample individualized education programs (IEPs) provided; select one IEP and review the Present Levels of Academic Achievement and Functional Performance (PLAAFP) section. Based on the PLAAFP, write 3–5 specific, measurable, attainable, results-oriented, and time-based (SMART) goals for the student. Once your goals are written, compare them to the goals included in the same IEP. Write a 1-page summary of this comparison, describing where the goals differ and why you think they might differ.

Data Collection Practice

1. Pick a TV show character to observe and then choose a behavior they exhibit that you believe should be targeted for change (*Super Nanny*, *Nanny 911*, *The Office*, *Big Bang Theory*, or *Scooby-Doo* are solid choices if you are having difficulty thinking of one). Write an operational definition for the chosen behavior and then collect data using an ABC data collection chart. Based on the data you collected, what is the hypothesis for a potential function of this behavior? Why did you choose that function?

Lesson Plans

1. After learning about the integral parts of a lesson, it is your turn to practice. Using the template provided, you will need to identify a subject and grade-level standard you want to teach to the class. Once this has been identified, you are to complete the lesson plan template. As you

are working through your project, ensure that you make note of where you are incorporating the UDL principles into the lesson.

Miscellaneous

1 **How-To Guide:** Your "How-To Guide" needs to be written in a book format. You may use Microsoft Word, but you can also use book programs such as Book Creator (https://bookcreator.com/). Your guide should be colorful and appealing and include images. Be creative and have fun. Try to think about this project as something you can give to teachers who may be new or who are struggling with meeting the varying needs of their students. Your book must be about disabilities in general, but you can break your book down into specific disabilities/strategies. Your book will need to be at a minimum 8–10 pages; this includes the examples you provide but does *not* include the cover page, table of contents, or reference page.

Things to include in your book:

- Cover page
- Table of contents
- Information on the following
    - Brain and learning (i.e., what parts of the brain are affecting learning and how)
    - Specific strategies that can be used in the classroom and how they can be integrated in lesson planning and delivery
    - Considerations for teachers as they plan for student learning
- Reference page (for the citations you use in your book)
    - You will need a **minimum of 3 references**, one of which can be your book.
    - You must include research support, which means you will need matching citations and references.
    - Follow APA for this.

2 **Classroom Website:** As a teacher, you will most likely be required to have a website where you can communicate with your parents and students. This project will help you begin to think about setting up your website. Granted, this project will focus on classroom management, but it can easily be adapted to fit the needs of your future classes. This

project will be time consuming, and I suggest you start early and keep working on it throughout the semester.

The following components need to be part of your website. You can find more detailed instructions on my sample website and/or on Blackboard.

1. Homepage
2. Philosophy of discipline
3. Newsletter
4. Classroom rules
5. Classroom procedures
6. Negative consequences
7. Substitute page
8. Classroom management/behavior resources
9. Data collection forms
10. References

Appendix C: ADA Compliance

We wanted to include this appendix as a reminder to everyone of the importance of being compliant with Title II of the Americans with Disabilities Act (ADA). We know that it is easy for us to get bogged down with the content and activities we need to plan for our online courses, which also means it is sometimes easy to forget that we also need to ensure that our courses are ADA compliant, meaning that all aspects of the course are accessible to all of our students with disabilities. While it has always been best practice to accommodate learning needs, it is also mandated by federal ruling. Effective June 2024, Title II of the ADA is requiring that institutes of higher education (IHEs) (and other government entities) have in place digital learning, including web and mobile-based apps that are appropriate and usable for all students.

While this book provided some different ways to look at instruction in the online classroom, you may have been thinking to yourself, well, what about our students with disabilities, including those who are neurodiverse—you never explicitly stated how we can support their unique needs. We strive to ensure that our courses are fully accessible, but there is so much that goes into accessibility and ADA compliance that was beyond the scope of this book (and should really be its own book). The most important advice we can give you is to be in contact with your IHE's compliance officer and your instructional design team. This ensures that you are being provided the most up-to-date information, and they can also help you with ensuring that your courses are accessible. Additionally, we want to mention the importance of following your students' accommodations. Many times by incorporating the Universal Design for Learning (UDL) framework, discussed in Appendix D and throughout the book, you will not have to make many adjustments to the course. However, it is still important that you are aware of and follow any accommodations you are provided. When in doubt, check with your disabilities accommodations personnel. Additionally, we would be remiss not to remind you that sometimes you need to make adjustments on the fly for your students. While we gave you a great number of instructional practices to incorporate into your classroom, we do understand that they are not all "just right" for every learner. When possible, and when it does not change the learning goal or standard, make adjustments to meet the needs of your students.

We know that not everyone reading this book has had students with disabilities in their classrooms, but from experience we can tell you that at some point in your online teaching career, you will. And you will likely find something in your course that may not be fully accessible to your students with disabilities. For example, Kathy has always received accommodations for her students who required them and would follow them. However, in all her years of teaching online, no student had ever before mentioned accessibility issues with virtual meetings. She had been using a program embedded into her learning management system (LMS) to host her virtual classes, without realizing it lacked closed-captioning and transcript options. Thanks to some students reaching out, she was able to quickly make a change for those two particular courses so that the live meeting and the recordings would be

---

Textbox C.1

Accessibility Suggestions

1 Add a description to any images you are using.
2 Use the closed-captioning feature when engaging in live virtual classes.
3 Use videos that already have closed-captioning embedded.
4 Use appropriate headings and formatting tools for written items so that a screen reader can read it.
5 Use sans serif fonts (e.g., Arial and Calibri) larger than 10 pt.
6 Use high contrast between background color and font color. Two examples would be black and white or blue font color on either white or black background.

accessible to them. She now uses the new program and always enables the closed-captioning option for her live courses, whether or not it is needed by any students. This is just one example of how you can easily implement accessibility features into your online courses. Textbox C.1 provides you with some other suggestions for ensuring your course is accessible. By having forethought and integrating these ideas on the front end, for when you do have students who need them, it will make your life easier than having to redo what you have already done. For those of you who are overwhelmed with ensuring your courses are accessible, the suggestions in Textbox C.1 are ones we have found the easiest to begin implementing.

Appendix D: Universal Design for Learning

The idea of online education is becoming more and more of a reality, and we are seeing our programs and courses growing, especially our alternative certification and graduate courses. Larger numbers of students taking online courses mean we will definitely see more diverse students in our classes. It is important that we meet the needs of all our students, no matter what the diversity. When we, the authors, think about diversity, we tend to look at the big picture—culture, language, ethnicity, socioeconomic status, neurodiversity and other disabilities, gender, religion, and the list goes on and on. While teaching to such a diverse population may seem overwhelming, we wanted to create this appendix to give you a framework that will help you meet the diverse students represented in your classroom. Throughout the book, we mentioned the Universal Design for Learning (UDL) framework but never specifically said what it was. This appendix will do just that, as well as provide information on UDL in higher education.

Many of you may be familiar with using the UDL framework in the PK–12 setting, but it is also an effective method used at the college/university level. By implementing the UDL framework, you will be able to meet most of the individual needs of your students in a proactive manner, rather than having to adjust in a reactive way. Many federal laws make reference to the use of UDL or ensuring that courses are accessible to all (e.g., the Americans with Disabilities Act [see Appendix C], Section 504 of the Rehabilitation Act). Specifically, the Higher Education Opportunity Act of 2008 recommends that institutes of higher education follow the UDL framework, stating that

> *UDL is a scientifically valid framework for guiding educational practice that (A) provides flexibility in the ways information is presented, in the ways students respond or demonstrate knowledge and skills, and in the ways students are engaged; and (B) reduces barriers in instruction, provides appropriate*

accommodations, supports and challenges, and maintains high achievement expectations for all students including students with disabilities and students who are limited English proficient. (HEOA, P.L. 110-315, §103[a][24])

At this point, you may be wondering what UDL is and how you incorporate it into your online classroom. Because we are passionate about UDL, almost the entire book provides ideas that align with the UDL framework. UDL is based on three principles: multiple means of engagement, multiple means of representation, and multiple means of action and expression. With multiple means of engagement, you are focusing on the "why" of learning. All of these guidelines are used to say that we must make our instruction relevant and help our students make connections with themselves and the content. The second UDL principle is multiple means of representation, or the "what" of learning. According to the CAST website, there are three guidelines that fall under representation. All in all, using multiple means of representation is all about representing different perspectives and ensuring that students have access to the materials in a way that is relevant and appropriate to them and their needs. The final principle, multiple means of action and expression, focuses on the "how" of learning. Within each of these principles and guidelines, CAST provides examples of what that might look like for you in your online courses. Please refer to the CAST (2024) reference for more information on these ideas in practice.

Many times we create our online instruction as a one-size-fits-all method, but with the diversity within each of our courses, this just will not work. Just as our PK–12 teachers must change instruction, we must also. While we know that there are specific standards that must be addressed, especially for our initial certification students, we also know that we are lucky—we can measure college students' knowledge in any way we want as long as it prepares them for whatever state requirements there are for certification. Throughout this book, we have discussed the idea of UDL and strongly believe that we need to teach this framework to our PK–12 educators, and the best way to do this is by modeling. By incorporating the UDL framework into your online classes, you are not following a one-size-fits-all approach; you are allowing your students to learn and demonstrate their knowledge in ways that best fit their individual needs, which will help prepare them to use this UDL framework in their own classes. One final note on implementing the UDL framework in your courses—do not try to do it all at once. This will only overwhelm you.

We both tell our students to start small and choose a module and/or one of the principles and start there; then continue to add as you are able.

References

Boothe, K. A., Lohmann, M. J., Donnell, K., & Hall, D. D. (2018). Applying the principles of Universal Design for Learning in the college classroom. *Journal of Special Education Apprenticeship, 7*(3), Article 2.

CAST. (2024). *Universal Design for Learning guidelines* (Version 3.0). https://udlguidelines.cast.org

Higher Education Opportunity Act. (2008). https://www.gpo.gov/fdsys/pkg/PLAW110publ315/pdf/PLAW-110publ315.pdf

Appendix E: Trauma-Informed Instruction in Higher Education

Over the past several years, we have heard a lot about the impact of trauma on learning and development for children. As teacher educators, we support our students in learning about trauma-informed practices so that they are better able to meet the needs of the children in their classroom. We discuss adverse childhood experiences (ACEs), which are traumatic events that occur in childhood and impact the long-term health of individuals (Bouiller & Blair, 2018). Almost 95% of university students report at least one ACE from their childhood (Kaminer et al., 2023), indicating that the vast majority of the students in our classrooms have experienced trauma at some point. And, post-COVID, it is likely that all students have experienced some trauma.

While trauma-informed instruction is not the focus of this book, we would be remiss if we did not at least mention the importance of considering this topic when planning instruction in your online classroom. The use of trauma-informed practices increases student perceptions of success in university courses, especially for students who report ACEs in their own childhoods (Lynch & Wojdak, 2023). In Textbox E.1, we offer a list of evidence-based trauma-informed online instructional practices. You will find that you are likely already doing at least some of these things, and others may be strategies we have suggested throughout the book. We highly recommend that you take the time to familiarize yourself with these trauma-informed instructional practices, research their use in your teaching area, and incorporate them into your courses. This appendix is not intended to provide you with all the information you need to be a trauma-informed teacher educator nor to offer a comprehensive list of practices. Instead, it is meant to remind you of the importance of considering trauma in your online classroom and get you thinking about changes to make in your instruction.

> **Textbox E.1**
>
> **Trauma-Informed Instructional Practices for Online Learning**
>
> - Awareness of the impact that adverse childhood experiences have on lifelong health and learning (Harper & Neubauer, 2021)
> - Well-structured and predictable classrooms that include clearly defined norms and expectations for all students and teachers (Kulikova & Maliy, 2017; Taylor, 2023)
> - Awareness of concepts taught in the course, or course activities, that may cause retraumatization (Anderson et al., 2023; Carello & Butler, 2014; Harper & Neubauer, 2021; Taylor, 2023)
> - Demonstrating empathy for student needs and concerns (Friedman, 2023; Marquart & Baez, 2021; Taylor, 2023)
> - Ensuring that students see the "human" side of their course instructor (Friedman, 2023)
> - Utilizing a variety of instructional strategies to teach and assess content in the course (Friedman, 2023)
> - Offering students choices, when appropriate (Marquart & Baez, 2021)
> - Explicitly teaching students about self-care and its importance in their own careers (Carello & Butler, 2015)
> - Connecting students with outside resources to support their physical and mental health needs, when appropriate (Carello & Butler, 2015)
> - Seeking student input on decisions related to classroom learning, when appropriate (Anderson et al., 2023)

References

Anderson, R. K., Landy, B., & Sanchez, V. (2023). Trauma-informed pedagogy in higher education: Considerations for the future of research and practice. *Practitioner and Theoretical Perspectives, 2*(2), 125–140. https://doi.org/10.32674/jis.v2i2.5012

Bouiller, M., & Blair, M. (2018). Adverse childhood experiences. *Paediatrics and Child Health, 28*(3), 132–137. https://doi.org/10.1016/j.paed.2017.12.008

Carello, J., & Butler, L. D. (2014). Potentially perilous pedagogies: Teaching trauma is not the same as trauma-informed teaching. *Journal of Trauma & Dissociation, 15*(2), 153–168. https://doi.org/10.1080/15299732.2014.867571

Carello, J., & Butler, L. D. (2015). Practicing what we teach: Trauma-informed educational practice. *Journal of Teaching in Social Work, 35*(3), 262–278. https://doi.org/10.1080/08841233.2015.1030059

Friedman, Z. I. (2023). Signature pedagogies versus trauma informed approaches: Thematic analysis of graduate students' reflections. *Pedagogy in Health Promotion, 9*(1), 17–26. https://doi.org/10.1177/23733799221118575

Harper, G. W., & Neubauer, L. C. (2021). Teaching during a pandemic: A model for trauma-informed education and administration. *Pedagogy in Health Promotion, 7*(1), 14–24. https://doi.org/10.1177/2373379920965596

Kaminer, D., Bravo, A. J., Mezquita, L., Pilatti, A., & Cross-Cultural Addictions Study Team. (2023). Adverse childhood experiences and adulthood mental health: A cross-cultural examination among university students in seven countries. *Current Psychology, 42*, 18370–18381. https://doi.org/10.1007/s12144-022-02978-3

Kulikova, T. I., & Maliy, D. V. (2017). Professional and personal qualities of the teacher in the context of the psychological safety of educational environment. *European Journal of Contemporary Education, 6*(4), 715–722.

Lynch, R. J., & Wojdak, K. (2023). An exploration of trauma-inclusive pedagogy and students' perceptions of academic success. *To Improve the Academy: A Journal of Educational Development, 42*(2), Article 6. https://doi.org/10.3998/tia.2634

Marquart, M., & Báez, J. C. (2021). Recommitting to trauma-informed teaching principles to support student learning: An example of a transformation in response to the Coronavirus pandemic. *Journal of Transformative Learning, 8*(1), 63–74.

Taylor, S. S. (2023). The need for trauma-informed care in higher education. *Educational Research: Theory and Practice, 34*(2), 86–94.

Appendix F: Artificial Intelligence in the Online Classroom

Artificial intelligence (AI)—we know that many of you see these words and your heart starts racing and full-on panic sets in. We also know that some of you are getting excited just to see those words and hear what we might have to say. AI has quickly become a central topic of conversation in the field of higher education, and many of us feel unprepared for its impact on our instruction, let alone for preparing our students to address AI-related issues in their own classrooms. When we proposed this book in 2023, AI was just beginning to be a conversation in the field, and we did not plan to even mention it in the book. However, as we wrote the book, the topic of AI had become important at most universities, and we felt we would be doing a disservice to you, the readers, if we did not at least acknowledge that we know that it is impacting your online instruction.

Like many of you, we are both actively trying to learn everything we can about AI and its implication for teacher education. Kathy is currently part of a book study on how PK–12 teachers use AI in their classrooms and has recently viewed several webinars on AI in both PK–12 and higher education classrooms. Marla has several books on AI on her desk and recently attended a virtual conference on the topic. The reality is that the more we learn about AI, the more we feel we don't know! We are both at the stage where we feel like we know just enough to be dangerous, so we are hesitant to give you much advice in this area. Below, we share some stories from our classrooms and ways we are addressing AI. But please understand that what we have included in this appendix is not an exhaustive list. And we know that this area is changing and evolving so quickly that anything we say may not be relevant by the time this book is in your hands.

For the most part, we are still trying to figure out how to deal with the use of AI and how it affects our students' schoolwork. This is something we have discussed at our universities, but it was not something we truly thought much about until the past year. We knew that students used websites where they could post their assignments and then other students could access them, which is one of many reasons we are adamant about making changes each time you teach a course, but AI takes this ability to cheat to a whole new level. Kathy remembers teaching classes in Summer 2024 when she noticed that several of her students were using words and sentence structures that did not match what she knew of those particular students, either from speaking to them in virtual meetings or office hours or even from their previous work. This is when she really began digging into AI and what she should do about it. For that course in particular, she had a talk with those students, some of whom said they had used Grammarly, which as many of you know will show up in AI detectors. Kathy now discusses the use of AI during her meeting with new graduate students and also includes a syllabus statement (see Textbox F.1).

Textbox F.1

Syllabus Statement

Use of Artificial Intelligence (ChaptGPT, tutor.com, Microsoft Gemini, etc.)

The integration of artificial intelligence (AI) into academic settings, particularly at the graduate level, presents both opportunities and challenges. While we know that the use of AI software is on the rise and is something you may be using in your own classroom, we strongly discourage its use for your assignments. Unless we specifically state that it is okay to use AI, please refrain. If you do choose to use AI for your assignments, please be aware of the academic integrity guidelines/consequences pertaining to plagiarism. Copying and pasting directly from AI sources without appropriate acknowledgment is considered plagiarism.

If you choose to use AI, please keep these points in mind:

- AI can reflect biases and inaccuracies at times. Fact-check and proofread your AI responses. Do not just assume it is giving you correct and legitimate information.

(Continued)

Textbox F.1 (Continued)

- Be cautious with data privacy. Do not input anything too personal or private. You cannot control where the information goes; how, when, or for how long the information is stored; or who will use it.
- Cite your use of AI using APA formatting.
- If you use websites such as Grammarly, AI detectors will find a higher percentage of AI-generated sentences.

Use AI to help:

1. Generate ideas for papers.
2. Edit your paper
3. Format references

Do NOT use AI for:

1. The entirety of a paper/assignment
2. The body of your paper
3. Locating sources for a paper or assignment

Note: This AI policy only applies to Dr. Boothe's courses. Other professors may have different rules or restrictions. Using AI without permission could violate academic integrity policies. Be sure to check specific guidelines for each class prior to AI use.

Note: The example above is a mixture of several different syllabus statements Kathy has seen floating around. This is by no means her sole creation. It takes a village to do what we do!

We both also see incredible value in using AI to support and enhance our own work. Marla's husband asked her how much AI support she was receiving in writing this book—the answer is none, but she can certainly see how it might have made the process a bit easier! Kathy has begun using AI to help create discussion prompts. In the discussion prompts, she also models how to cite the use of AI and let readers (or in this case students) know how to cite and how to use it properly. She wants students to be aware that she knows what

AI can do, but she also wants them to learn how to use it appropriately since we know it can be a valuable tool in their learning.

We previously mentioned AI detectors, such as TurnItIn and PlagiarismCheck, which are embedded into many learning management systems (LMSs). We caution you to be careful when using these tools to identify students who used AI for their coursework, as the tools often are not accurate. In our experience, many online instructors see the score in the detection software and automatically assume the student used AI, instead of actually reviewing the report. According to Weber-Wulff et al. (2023), AI detectors can mislabel student course submissions at a rate of 80%. So, as much as we would like to say stay away from the AI detectors, we do believe there is value in them, as long as you also use common sense and know your students. If you have the benefit of having the same students in multiple courses, you can compare current assignment submissions to previous work (and we highly recommend doing so).

We have talked to several instructors who are trying to embrace AI in their classes since they know their students are using it in their own schools. Textbox F.2 provides some examples of ways you can incorporate AI into

---

Textbox F.2

Artificial Intelligence Course Activity Ideas

1 Have AI create an essay about themselves or their hometown. Then have them fact-check the essay and compare and contrast the two. Share with peers in a discussion post. Have students complete a form that states how they used AI for their assignment as well as providing the prompt they used and the AI results.

2 With the example above, you can also provide students with a range of acceptable AI use for each assignment. Make sure you give examples of what each level looks like. For example, Level 1 = Disallowed, Level 2 = Restricted, Level 3 = Documented, and Level 4 = Unrestricted (Hargrave et al., 2024).

(Continued)

Textbox F.2 (Continued)

3 Have AI give you discussion prompts over specific topics. From our experience, they need to be edited and manipulated to make it work for your particular content and grade.

4 Have AI create a presentation based on information you input.

5 Create lesson plans. Submit both the prompt you gave the AI, as well as the lesson plan that was created.

Textbox F.3

Artificial Intelligence Tools

AI Tool
Google Gemini
MagicSchool AI
Grammarly
Brisk Teaching
Curipod

---

your online courses, while Textbox F.3 provides AI tools you may find helpful if you are still learning about AI. We did not include the hyperlinks to these AI tools because we know that these change often, but a simple Google search should pull them up for you.

Finally, below are some things to keep in mind when you or your students plan to use AI for university coursework in the PK–12 classroom.

1 Understand the importance of not using any personal information when writing prompts into AI—no student names, school names, grades, etc.

2 Do your own research and use common sense—AI programs may give inaccurate or biased information based on their algorithms. They also do not always understand the entire prompt you give them, so they may not give you the full answer or may give you a wrong answer.

3 Do not use AI as the only tool for completing or creating assignments—use it as a helpful tool to brainstorm or improve existing work. The actual work of thinking and creating learning materials needs to be done by a human, not by an AI tool.

The topic of artificial intelligence in the classroom is an ever-evolving topic, and we would definitely love to hear from you about how you incorporate AI into your online courses, as well as how you prepare your students for AI in their own classrooms. Please share on social media using the hashtag #OnlineTeacherPrep and tagging us.

References

Hargrave, M., Fisher, D., & Frey, N. (2024). *The artificial intelligence playbook: Time-saving tools for teachers that make learning more engaging*. Corwin.

Weber-Wulff, D., Anohina-Naumeca, A., Bjelobaba, S., Foltynek, T., Guerrero-Dib, J., Popoola, O., Sigut, P., & Waddington, L. (2023). Testing of detection tools for AI-generated text. *International Journal of Educational Integrity, 1*(19). https://doi.org/10.48550/arXiv.2306.15666

Appendix G: Our Favorite Things

After almost a decade of teaching online and working remotely, we have created a list of our favorite things (anyone else singing the song from *The Sound of Music* in their head right now?). Some of you may already have your list of must-haves for online teaching, but for those of you new to this instructional format, we want to share our recommendations for what online teacher educators need to succeed.

1. **A not-too-heavy laptop.** You will likely have a mobile office at times, whether that is to work from your favorite coffee shop or simply from the couch. In addition, you will be attending conferences and presenting to schools—you don't want a backache from carrying your laptop from place to place!

2. **A second (or third) monitor.** There will be times when you need to see a lot of information at once, such as when you need to see the assignment instructions and rubric while you grade. This is much simpler when you can view the information on multiple screens. Marla highly recommends a portable monitor that can easily slide into your laptop bag along with your computer.

3. **An external webcam.** We suspect your laptop will have a decent webcam. But, inevitably, it won't work one day. And that will certainly be a day on which you have to teach class and have virtual student meetings scheduled. Prepare for this unfortunate day by purchasing an external webcam. You don't need anything fancy, and we don't recommend spending much.

4. **A headset.** Similar to the webcam, you will unexpectedly need this one day when your laptop audio suddenly stops working. Be prepared! In addition, if you have noisy children or dogs at home, the headset helps

block out the noise so that your students (and you) hear less of that noise during class.

5. **A ring light.** It can be hard to get the lighting "just right" for recording videos and teaching class. Most of us don't have perfect lighting in our home offices. The ring light helps to direct the light exactly where you need it to improve video quality.

6. **A comfy chair.** You will be at your desk for long stretches of time. Online teaching is hard work and requires a lot of sitting. Make sure you have a chair that provides good ergonomic support.

7. **Notepads and Post-It notes.** Yes, you are teaching online and can technically write everything on your computer. But trust us—there will be times when you will want to write yourself a quick reminder note about a student need or a change to make in a course.

8. **Cute pens or other writing utensils.** You must have something to use for writing on those notepads! We highly suggest having a selection of pens that make you smile (those of you who are former elementary school teachers will likely want a set of colorful flair pens).

9. **Dry erase board.** While this is a great idea for a work office, we have also found that it is helpful in our home office to keep track of our work life. Kathy has a dry erase board that has sections for conference proposals, changes that need to be made to future courses, writing projects that are currently being worked on, writing projects that are under review, and even a section for future writing ideas. She also puts a reminder on there of the days and times of her office hours and classes (the older you get and the more you multitask, the more you need that).

10. **Good snacks.** We firmly believe that good snacks and our favorite beverages make us better teacher educators. So stock up on those snacks! In Kathy's office, you will find Diet Coke and candy, while Marla's office is well stocked with coffee, Dr. Pepper Zero, and peanut butter M&M's. While these are all unhealthy snacks, sometimes they are what gets us through the day, especially grading days!

11. **Trusted friends.** Like any job, there will be hard days. You need at least a few trusted friends you can call to make you laugh and listen to your worries.

Appendix H: Additional Resources We Recommend

This appendix is all about our favorite resources. The resources we included are broken down by medium and cover all topics we discuss in this book—UDL, AI, authentic assessment, etc. While we do include web links in this appendix, we also know technology and links change. Hopefully a simple Google search will get you near a new and improved website if the ones we include do not work.

Articles

Bartlett, M. J., Arslan, F. N., Bankston, A., & Sarabipour, S. (2021). Ten simple rules to improve academic work-life balance. *PLOS Computational Biology, 17*(7), e1009124. https://doi.org/10.1371/journal.pcbi.1009124

Boothe, K. A., & Lohmann, M. J. (2024). Modeling and encouraging self-care in online teacher preparation: Lessons learned during the COVID-19 pandemic. *Networks: An Online Journal for Teacher Research, 25*(1). https://doi.org/10.4148/2470-6353.1376

Boothe, K. A., Lohmann, M. J., Donnell, K., & Hall, D. D. (2018). Applying the principles of Universal Design for Learning in the college classroom. *Journal of Special Education Apprenticeship, 7*(3), Article 2.

Boothe, K. A., Lohmann, M. J., & Owiny, R. L. (2020). Enhancing student learning in the online instructional environment through the use of Universal Design for Learning. *Networks: An Online Journal for Teacher Research, 22*(1). https://doi.org/10.4148/2470-6353.1310

Hamadi, H., Tafili, A., Kates, F. R., Larson, S. A., Ellison, C., & Song, J. (2023). Exploring an innovative approach to enhance discussion board engagement. *TechTrends: For Leaders in Education & Training, 67*, 741–751. https://doi.org/10.1007/s11528-023-00850-0

Lendak-Kabok, K. (2022). Women's work-life balance strategies in academia. *Journal of Family Studies, 28*(3), 1139–1157. https://doi.org/10.1080/13229400.2020.1802324

Lohmann, M. J., & Boothe, K. A. (2022). Using asynchronous discussions to teach classroom management skills in online teacher preparation courses. *Journal of Special Education Preparation, 2*(3), 48–58.

Lohmann, M. J., & Boothe, K. A. (2024). Supporting student engagement through the use of three discussion formats in a graduate teacher education course. *Journal of the American Academy of Special Education Professionals*, Winter, Article 3.

Lohmann, M. J., Boothe, K. A., Hathcote, A. R., & Turpin, A. (2018). Engaging graduate students in the online learning environment: A Universal Design for Learning (UDL) approach to teacher preparation. *Networks: An Online Journal for Teacher Research, 20*(2). https://doi.org/10.4148/2470-6353.1264

Lupu, I., & Ruiz-Castro, M. (2021, January 29). Work-life balance is a cycle, not an achievement. *Harvard Business Review*. https://hbr.org/2021/01/work-life-balance-is-a-cycle-not-an-achievement

Shauger, R., Boothe, K. A., & Lohmann, M. J. (2023). Creativity in the virtual classroom: Engaging online special education teacher candidates in their own learning. *Journal of Special Education Apprenticeship, 12*(2), 47–63.

Books

Alaniz, K., & Cerling, K. (2023). *Authentic assessment in action: An everyday guide for bringing learning to life through meaningful assessment*. Rowman & Littlefield.

Blum, S. D. (Ed.). (2020). *Ungrading: Why rating students undermines learning (and what to do instead)*. West Virginia University Press.

Boothe, K. A., & Hathcote, A. R. (2021). *A case study approach to writing individualized special education documents: From preschool to graduation*. Council for Exceptional Children.

Ceglie, R., Thornburg, A., & Abernathy, D. (Eds.). (2020). *Handbook of research on developing engaging online courses*. IGI Global.

Irish, C., & Davis, J. (Eds.). (2021). *Lessons from the pivot: Higher education's response to the pandemic*. College of Education Books. https://scholar.umw.edu/education_books/1

Jarvie, S., & Metz, C. (Eds.). (2024). *Balance and boundaries in creating meaningful relationships in online higher education*. IGI Global.

Lohmann, M. J. (2023). *The teacher's guide to action research for special education in PK–12 classrooms*. Rowman & Littlefield.

Murawski, W., & Scott, K. L. (2019). *What really works with Universal Design for Learning*. Corwin.

Novak, K. (2022). *UDL Now! A teacher's guide to applying Universal Design for Learning*. CAST.

Urgolo-Huchvale, M., & McNeal, K. (Eds.). (2023). *Engaging students with disabilities in remote learning environments*. IGI Global.

Organizations

American Association of Colleges for Teacher Education—https://aacte.org
Association of Teacher Educators—https://www.ate1.org
Council for Exceptional Children—https://exceptionalchildren.org

Webinars

CAST. (2024). *Guidelines 3.0 and adult education: Enhancing inclusivity and success.* https://www.cast.org/products-services/events/2024/08/guidelines-3.0-career-technical-education-enhancing-inclusivity-success

Websites

Center for Applied Special Technology (CAST)—https://www.cast.org
Center for Innovation, Design, and Digital Learning—https://ciddl.org
Quality Matters—https://www.qualitymatters.org

Index

Americans with Disabilities Act (ADA) 201
announcements 18
Artificial Intelligence (AI) 5, 210
assessment 5
    authentic assessment 5, 107
    formative assessment 107
    grading assessments 132
    myths about assessment 107
    rubrics for assessments 132
    self-assessment 23
    student assessments for faculty self-reflection 154
    summative assessment 108
author positionality 1

beliefs about teaching and learning 2

choice 15
collaborative learning 22
    collaborative assignments/work 45, 110
community
    benefits of online learning communities 36
    community building tools 48
    myths about community building 35

disability
discussions
    asynchronous 22
    discussion reflection post 64
    expectations for discussions 60
    facilitating discussion boards 59
    myths about discussion boards 57
    varied discussion formats 59, 66
diverse needs 26

emergency remote teaching 86
engagement
    myths about engagement 11
    student engagement 13

feedback
    feedback and grading assessments 133
    regular and substantive feedback 6, 76
    specific feedback 136
    varied feedback tools 137
flipped classroom 23

instructional tools 16
    tools for assessment 111
    tools for building community 36, 48
    tools for feedback 137
    tools for supporting student engagement 25
    tools for remote observation 88
    tools for self-reflection 151
instructor presence 19

learning styles 3
lifelong learners 3

modeling 3
motivation
    intrinsic motivation 13, 14
myths 4
    myths about community 35
    myths about engaging learners 11

office hours 21

remote observation 85
    FERPA and remote observation 87
    guidelines for remote observation 93
    student expectations for remote observation 89
rubrics 133

self-reflection 88
    myths about self reflection 147
social media 41
    Facebook 44
    Twitter/X 42
synchronous meetings 44

trauma-informed instruction 207

universal design for learning 6, 204
    multiple means of action and expression 110, 205
    multiple means of engagement 16, 205
    multiple means of representation 205
    universally designed classroom 3

work-life balance 167

About the Authors

Dr. Kathleen A. Boothe is an associate professor and program coordinator of special education at Southeastern Oklahoma State University, where she currently teaches fully online to both graduate and undergraduate students. Dr. Boothe has taught asynchronous online teacher education courses since 2015, averaging approximately sixteen courses per academic year. Dr. Boothe is an active member of the Council for Exceptional Children's Teacher Education Division. Dr. Boothe's research interests include improving online education for pre- and in-service teachers, with a focus on Universal Design for Learning (UDL). She has published several book chapters and articles on effective online teaching in higher education. In 2020, Dr. Boothe received the Faculty Senate Recognition Award for Outstanding Research and Scholarly Activity. Most recently, Dr. Boothe received the Faculty Senate Recognition Award for Excellence in Teaching for the 2024–2025 school year.

You can find Kathy on Twitter/X at @kah1978.

Dr. Marla J. Lohmann is an associate professor and program director of special education and alternative licensure at Colorado Christian University. She teaches fully online undergraduate and graduate general and special education coursework and currently teaches about thirty-six credit hours per academic year. Dr. Lohmann is an active member of the Council for Exceptional Children's Teacher Education Division at both the state and international levels. She is passionate about offering high-quality pre-service teacher preparation and ongoing training for in-service teachers in the virtual university classroom. Dr. Lohmann has taught more than 130 asynchronous online teacher education courses and was awarded the 2018 CCU Colorado Christian University Curriculum & Instruction Division Outstanding Faculty Member Award based on student nomination and feedback.

You can find Marla on Twitter/X at @MarlaLohmann.